What Others Are Saying

"Marc has written a powerful, practical book that can transform your sales results and give you a real edge in today's market."
Brian Tracy - Bestselling Author of The Psychology of Selling

"When I read a sales book, I look for a couple of nuggets that will give me a competitive edge. I found a bucket of gold in *Game Plan Selling*."
Bill Cates - Author of Get More Referrals Now

"If you have ever played sports and need to master selling, then you will love this book. *Game Plan Selling* shows us how to be a champion in the sport of sales."
Jim Tunney - Former NFL Referee, "The Dean of NFL Refs"

"In the old days, salespeople were in power because they had information buyers needed. Today, buyers are in charge because everything they need to research products, services, and companies is freely available on the web. New selling models are required. Are you playing by the new rules? Marc Wayshak shows you how."
David Meerman Scott - Bestselling author of The New Rules of Marketing and PR

"These strategies work. Selling has never been a gentle sport, but these times require a flawless system. Wayshak provides us with just that; Loved it, so today!"
Robert Goodwin - Former CEO of Insta-Care Pharmacy Services

"Most entrepreneurs don't succeed because they don't know how to effectively sell, this book lays out a sales system that is easy to follow, that will help you close more deals ethically without ever seeming salesy and that will help you build deeper relationships. If you need a new approach that will work, read this book."
Arel Moodie - Bestselling Author & Inc. Magazine 30 Under 30 Honoree

"If you are looking to close more sales then this book is a must-read. Marc Wayshak provides a great new perspective on and a lot of usable solutions to one of the oldest challenges in selling--closing the deal."
Suzanne Bates - Bestselling Author of Speak Like a CEO

"Marc Wayshak has worked with my team for years and his systematic and disciplined approach has been a critical component to our success. If you want to increase your sales, don't just read this book, apply everything that's in it."
Paul Marsan - President of Carpenter & Costin Landscape Management

"*Game Plan Selling* shows us, in a very fun-to-read style, exactly how to close the sale in a time when the rules of selling have changed."
John Chapin - Author of the Gold-Medal Winning SALES ENCYCLOPEDIA

"If you want to learn how to close business deals in today's market, this comprehensive sales guide will put you ahead of the curve."
Dan Schawbel - Founder of Millennial Branding & Author of Me 2.0

"As a competitor and business owner, I know that the more systematic I become - the better my results tend to be. That's the first of a dozen reasons why I'd recommend *Game Plan Selling*. From the broader understandings of trends in the sales world, to plug-and-play tips for making calls and building relationships, this book will do good for any serious salesperson."
Daniel Faggella - National Brazilian Jiu Jitsu Champion and Owner at Black Diamond Mixed Martial Arts

GAME PLAN SELLING

The Definitive Rulebook for Closing the Sale in the Age of the Well-Informed Prospect

Marc Wayshak

Dedication

This book is dedicated to my family, the motivation behind every sale I've ever made.

Contents

Claim Your Free MP3

As a special bonus for investing in this book I'd like to give you access to a special one-hour audio program, developed to supplement the material in this book. It's packed with information about how to immediately implement Game Plan Selling into your career and will enhance the value of the book you are now holding in your hands. Just go to www.GamePlanSellingGift.com to claim your free MP3. (You'll also receive my weekly e-mail Sales Tips as another bonus.)

You'll discover:

- Why being distinct from everyone else is the key to explosive sales growth in today's market
- How to instantly set yourself apart from the competition in the eyes of your prospects
- How to connect with your prospects
- How to become a systematic seller
- How to gain the respect of your prospects so they stop hiding, cheating and stealing from you
- How to give unforgettable presentations that prompt immediate decisions from your prospects
- How to create your own prospecting plan that will guarantee the achievement of your sales goals
- How to sell more than you ever have before

Claim your free bonus MP3 at: www.GamePlanSellingGift.com

CHAPTER 1

Introduction

In today's technology-driven world, information is cheap. The Internet has changed everything for prospects. No longer do they need the big sales pitch explaining all of the features and benefits of a product. There's a

---

Rule #1: In the age of the well-informed prospect, information selling is dead.

---

website for that—and probably many of them. 98% of Americans with a total household income of over $75,000 use the Internet. Of the Internet users, 78% look for information online about a service or product they are thinking of buying.[1] Prospects are savvier

---

[1] Pew Internet & American Life Project

than ever, now that they're armed with so much information on our products and services.

There was a time when it was a salesperson's job to provide information, but that's simply no longer the case. A salesperson's job now entails helping prospects identify whether they're the right fit for a particular product or service.

This is why I've developed a new way of looking at selling; the game has changed, and so must the rules. Salespeople have been struggling with a changing sales environment over the past twenty years. In all that time, there have been no viable alternatives to information selling.

Since I began helping companies deal with their sales challenges, I have found myself constantly drawing on my experiences as an athlete to come up with solutions. As an All-American and Harvard Rugby Team Captain, I learned to confidently navigate a field of competitors by being distinct, develop repeatable strategies, and execute a plan with commitment and passion. The comparison with sales is obvious. With the right strategy and the right attitude, victory is possible in sales and sports alike.

My sales method is called Game Plan Selling because today's successful sales team—like the starting line-up on any championship team—needs to know the rules, develop its own unique strategy, and follow through with the plan to achieve its goals.

This book will walk you through three core principles known as the *Game Plan Selling DSP* to help close the sale by being:

- ➤ **Distinct** from the competition, being

- ➤ **Systematic** for every aspect of selling, and having a

- ➤ Prospecting **Playbook** to live by.

Within each section are rules you can apply immediately to your selling career. You will learn how to separate yourself from the competition by being completely unique from others in your field. You will learn to follow a simple system to close larger sales with greater frequency in any selling situation. And, finally, you will learn how to create and follow a selling plan that will allow you to achieve so much more by eliminating fear and doubt over achieving your sales and personal goals.

As you begin this process to improve your sales, you will undoubtedly face moments of uncertainty and trepidation. It can be difficult to step out of your comfort zone and learn a new and better way to sell. But if you're willing to take those first steps outside of your normal sales routine, you will discover a world of selling success that you otherwise may never have known.

This is a personal journey as well as a professional one—I learned early on that success in sales is all about meeting personal goals. The more you sell, the more you can afford to have what you need and want in life. The only question is whether you have the determination to see the journey through.

By simply reading this book, you have already joined an elite group of people: those who are willing to face their weaknesses, open their eyes, and explore what is possible beyond the status quo. Congratulations on taking your first step toward the excellence that accompanies Game Plan Selling!

I want you to know how happy I am that you're investing your time in this book. I want you to succeed and experience what's out there beyond old-school selling techniques. And when you do, please share your thoughts, stories and experiences with me as well as share a copy with a friend or colleague.

To supplement the value of this book, don't forget to visit www.GamePlanSellingGift.com for your free MP3 to follow up on key concepts and sign up for my free e-mail Sales Tips. Also, be sure to contact me at that same website if you have any questions about my sales coaching programs for salespeople and entrepreneurs, my sales training for companies or my speaking programs for associations and corporate functions.

Here's to successful Game Plan Selling,

Marc Wayshak

CHAPTER 2

How I Fell Into Sales

"Marc, your college fund has shrunk significantly over the past three months…"

......

U p until my nineteenth birthday, the wind had been at my back. I grew up in a small suburban community outside of Boston with a caring family. I had a lovable and devoted golden retriever that I would walk regularly at the pond behind my house. I was always a three-season athlete in high school and studied hard.

When the time for college came, I was fortunate enough to earn a spot at Harvard University, where I expected sports, fun and some studying to be my way of life. However, during the winter of my freshman year of college, I received a phone call that forever changed the course of my life.

Every few months I would receive updates about the money I had invested in the stock market. This large sum of money was supposed to pay for my college tuition over the next three-and-a-half years. Thanks to some explosive stock growth over the course of my childhood, a small sum of money invested by my parents had grown exponentially by the time I was ready for college.

This call, however, turned my reality upside down. What was once enough money to pay for all of college was now not even enough to get me through to the end of my freshman year. Like many others, I had just lost my savings to a stock market crash.

This sudden need to contribute to paying for our college tuition spurred my brother and me to start a business. During our search for a business idea, we came across a company looking to sell some promotional equipment. The equipment included giant inflatable characters, hot dog stands, moon bounces and search lights that we could use for "grand opening" celebrations at retail stores.

A flyer given to prospects during sales meetings in the early years.

We took out a loan from a local bank, bought the equipment and instantly became young entrepreneurs. It was exciting, but we were clueless. I somehow expected business to start pouring in once we opened shop. That wasn't the case.

I quickly realized I would have to learn to sell if our business was going to succeed.

I decided to go out to local convenience stores and meet with the owners. I thought I would just sell our services to them and we'd be rich! I didn't even ask for anyone's advice on how to sell because I *knew* it would be easy.

I'll never forget that first taste of being a salesman. I would walk into a convenience store and ask for the owner. If the owner were there, I would tell him what we could do to increase sales with our promotion. Usually, within the first thirty seconds the owner would cut me off and tell me to leave—if he was in a good mood. After the first three attempts, I became discouraged. I didn't like this rejection. But I was committed, so I stuck with it—each time with no success.

With each subsequent rejection, I became more nervous and shy when approaching the owners. I had been told to "screw off" by one gas station owner. Another told me that he would talk to me after he finished up with a phone call—his phone call lasted for two hours while I waited with excitement in the parking lot. As soon as he hung up, he snuck out the back door.

My favorite experience in that first week was when I actually got the opportunity to give my presentation to a gas station owner and, in my fit of excitement, I suddenly couldn't remember what to say. After that first week, I had stopped in at fifty gas stations and hadn't made a single sale. It was a disaster. I wanted it to end.

Finally, I went to my father, who had been a career salesman, and told him that I didn't think I was cut out for sales.

"I'm just not the 'sales-type,'" I said.

"Well, you're going to have to learn to sell if you want to make this work," he replied.

"I don't think I have the right personality for selling, though," I complained.

In that conversation, I remember him saying, "Selling is a skill, not an innate talent that you either have or don't have." With that, I decided to invest a little money in some of the classic selling technique books. I suddenly became inspired by the possibilities of learning to become a great salesman. I committed to doing whatever it took to learn to sell. I read every book I could find on the subject, and I began to see that they generally told me the same three things:

1. Persuade prospects by pitching your product with a smile and a fancy suit,

2. Selling is a game of intuition, enthusiasm and instinct, and

3. The law of attraction will bring you sales if you create a nice brochure, make some cold calls and develop strong word-of-mouth.

Armed with this *knowledge* and new-found confidence, I would bring my "pitch book" to whatever prospecting meetings I was lucky enough to stumble across. I would then proceed to put on the greatest "dog and pony show" they'd ever seen. Wearing the sharpest suit I could afford with fake reading glasses (to make me look more sophisticated!), I would impress them with great visuals, charm them with my rehearsed smile and close with a strong question like, "What else do you need to see right now to sign on the dotted line?"

It was magical! Prospects would tell me how great a salesman I was. They would compliment me on my presentation.

They would thank me for all of the incredible information. One prospect even told me that he thought I "could sell ice to an Eskimo." (I was so proud!)

But these people all had one thing in common: they didn't buy.

After doing the same thing for a few years, I got very frustrated. To be clear, our business did grow during those years — thanks mostly to some lucky opportunities and sheer willpower. And they were exciting years even with the frustration. Over the course of four years I built a business while earning a college degree, leading the Harvard Rugby Team as its captain and being honored as an All-American athlete. Then, suddenly, it was all over.

After graduation, the excitement waned; I was left with increasing pressure to sell more. I had to turn around an underperforming business and I knew there had to be a better way to increase our sales.

➢ Why couldn't I find more prospects?

➢ What was causing some of my best prospects to suddenly disappear on me?

➢ Why were customers beating me down on price?

➢ How come prospects would tell me one thing and then go do another?

By this point, I was calling the same list of fifty prospects each month. I made follow-up call after follow-up call, asking if anything had changed. Nothing ever did.

Then something truly life-changing happened to me. I found a group of mentors that saw sales from a completely different perspective. These true sales experts saw everything the opposite way. And, slowly, selling began to make sense to me. I could see why I had the challenges I did.

Here's how it began: one fateful March afternoon, I paid $10,000 on my credit card, to join an intensive sales coaching program and set out to learn everything that I possibly could. Over the next few months, I became obsessed with learning every selling technique that they had to offer. After their trainings, I would go home and type up every single script, line or concept I could glean from their wisdom. It was all so different from what I had learned up until then.

I loved it.

Within six months, my business was in a totally different place. I landed some major new clients, including Subway Sandwich Shops and Getty Petroleum, thanks to what I had learned.

After another six months, we received an offer to sell to a competitor of ours. After much negotiation, we took the offer and, at twenty-three years old — following my passion to master modern selling — I went on to become one of the youngest sales trainers in America.

During that next year, I trained organizations large and small, experimenting with my own techniques while continuing to research and interview some of the top salespeople in a range of industries.

Now that I understood that selling wasn't about a persuasive pitch, intuition and the law of attraction, I began to understand what the best salespeople out there were really doing.

Moreover, the techniques which worked began to remind me more and more of my experiences playing competitive sports.

Selling wasn't just a game, it was a very competitive one, where the top 5% of salespeople out-earn the other 95%.

Over the years and throughout the process of honing my sales method, I realized I had a unique selling technique based on three core principles—or, the *Game Plan Selling DSP*, which helped me close sales by being:

- ➢ **Distinct** from the competition, being

- ➢ **Systematic** for every aspect of selling, and having a

- ➢ Prospecting **Playbook** to live by.

CHAPTER 3

Why Read This Book

The 31 Most Common Struggles in Sales

D o you and/or your sales team struggle with some of these issues?

1. Can't get through to C-level people
2. Not reaching decision makers
3. Being outsold by the competition
4. Competing mostly on price
5. Sales cycle is too long
6. Losing too many sales
7. Losing business to low-priced competitors
8. Dealing with unqualified leads
9. Dealing with prospects that can't afford you
10. Prospects that are "thinking it over" disappear
11. Wasting time on prospects that go nowhere
12. Getting shopped around
13. Inconsistent sales results
14. Too busy to manage your sales load
15. Salespeople aren't closing the business

16. Not prospecting enough for new opportunities
17. Salespeople don't have a clear sales process
18. Increased competition
19. Down economy is hurting margins
20. Salespeople are busy but not productive
21. Salespeople are professional visitors and order-takers
22. Give prospects quotes, never to hear back
23. Salespeople struggle to sell on value
24. Lack motivation within the sales team
25. Not many "A" players on the sales team
26. Reluctant to make new sales calls
27. Would be in serious trouble if lost number-one client
28. Not sure what to say in sales meetings
29. Tend to speak most of the time in sales meetings
30. Prospecting calls simply are not working
31. Not getting enough referrals

If you said yes to any of these challenges, it's probably due to one or more of these three issues:

1. Prospects perceive you as like other salespeople and therefore "salesy,"

2. You lack a systematic sales game plan, and

3. You don't have a clear day-to-day Prospecting Playbook to follow in order to be successful.

The *Game Plan Selling DSP* is designed to help you deal with the issues above by being:

> **Distinct** from the competition, being

> **Systematic** for every aspect of selling, and having a

> Prospecting **Playbook** to live by.

Within this book are many ideas that you can implement immediately. I challenge you to implement as many as possible. The key to everything that I present is that I give you a simple and easy-to-use system. You have 900 other things to worry about— "how you sell" should not be one of them. By using this system, you will no longer have to think about what to do next. All you have to do is follow the system.

The Game Plan Selling DSP

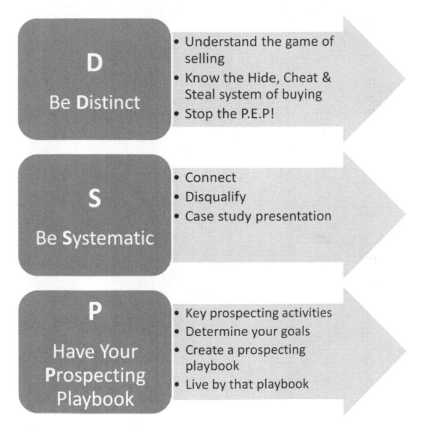

D

Be Distinct

- Understand the game of selling
- Know the Hide, Cheat & Steal system of buying
- Stop the P.E.P!

S

Be Systematic

- Connect
- Disqualify
- Case study presentation

P

Have Your Prospecting Playbook

- Key prospecting activities
- Determine your goals
- Create a prospecting playbook
- Live by that playbook

BE DISTINCT

...From the Competition

CHAPTER 4

Be Distinct from the Competition

W hen I first learned to sell, most sales trainers had the same advice: "Persuade prospects by

---

Rule #2: When you are perceived to be like every other salesperson, the protective walls of the prospect go up.

---

pitching your product with a smile and a fancy suit!" You might think I'm exaggerating, but I'm not. This is what most of the sales literature out there says to do.

In reality, this approach sends up red flags in the mind of the prospect. A sales style dominated by persuasion sounds like this: "I'm going to throw up on you with all of my information, even though you don't know if you need, want or have any use for what I have to say. And I'm going to do it with a slick, inauthentic style so you won't trust me."

ARE YOU THROWING UP ON YOUR PROSPECTS?

Client Case Study:

I once worked with a high-end hotel that struggled with sales despite having an intelligent and charming sales staff. The staff had been trained by an old-school sales trainer to smile a lot, use fancy PowerPoint presentations, turn on the charm and give re-hearsed pitches based on some preliminary probing questions. The result was that they were simply not closing deals — and the deals they did close were won through very competitive pricing.

When I met with the general manager of the hotel, he explained that he just didn't understand what the problem was. His salespeople would often get positive feedback from prospects about how they were treated, and everyone on his staff had "the gift of gab."

When I asked to see a sales pipeline of prospects they intended to close, he showed me a long document full of prospective sales. The general manager felt optimistic about that — but, after some more digging, I explained to him what was really going on.

By doing all of the things they were doing — giving rehearsed PowerPoint pitches based on little information; being insincerely smiley and friendly; trying to persuade prospects rather than understand them — the sales staff were acting like all the other salespeople the prospects had ever met. It's not that this stuff is inherently wrong; it's just extremely common. When they were perceived to be like every other sales team out there, that high-end hotel instantly had no more value to the prospect than a group of people begging for money.

There was a time when these old-school sales techniques worked — about seventy years ago, when they were first developed. Back then, prospects were not used to the "salesy" approach, they had little access to information on products and they had much more time to spare without all of the distractions in today's society.

Rule #3: Times are different in today's market and salespeople must adapt or die.

Today, prospects are fully prepared to defend themselves from the pitch—in fact, they're increasingly investing in training courses designed to help buyers extract the most value from salespeople. Prospects have limitless access to information—no longer are they dependent on salespeople to access information on products and services. And prospects are busier than ever, so they don't have time to be interrupted for a lengthy sales pitch. The average corporate employee has well over a full week of work piled up on the desk right now. Times are different in the today's market and salespeople must adapt or die.

CHAPTER 5

The Game of Selling

Whether or not you purposely sell with a system, prospects will always buy with a system. The system they'll use has a name: The Hide, Cheat and Steal system of buying.

Here's how it works:

Prospects will hide from salespeople they deem low-value by any means necessary in order to avoid a direct confrontation.

Rule #4: Whether or not you sell with a system, prospects will always buy with a system.

For instance, one of my clients recently told me how a prospect's assistant told him that the prospect was going to be out sick for a few weeks. My client sent him a get-well card right away.

Two weeks later, my client saw that same prospect at an industry meeting. My client went up to the prospect and asked how he was feeling. The prospect had no idea what my client was talking about...

The reality is that many of us are probably guilty of this ourselves when we buy, so ask yourself why you do it. It's probably because you perceive the salesperson to be of little value to you and fear he will try to use some fancy headlock closing technique to get you to buy.

Imagine playing a sport against an opponent you know is cheating, but instead of doing anything about it, you simply play game after game, losing each time because the opponent cheated. It seems unimaginable, but salespeople allow it to happen all the time.

Think of all the times you had a sales meeting, at the end of which you scheduled a follow-up call, only never to hear from the prospect again. Knowing what I know now, I do not understand why salespeople continue to put up with this.

Prospects steal from salespeople all the time. There is information that prospects want, and would readily pay for in the form of consulting (Boston Consulting Group, just down the street

---

Rule #5: Prospects will cheat in order to gain any advantage with salespeople.

---

from where I live, brought in over $3 billion last year), but we foolish salespeople give it away day after day in the hopes that something will come back in return. Would you share your playbook with the other team before a big game? I doubt it.

Rule #6: Most salespeople will jump at the opportunity to be abused and cheated by the prospect. Don't let it happen to you.

What salespeople are really doing is lowering their perceived value to the prospect by giving away all of their high-value information for free. And salespeople are willing to do it over and

THE UNFAIR, TUG-O-WAR GAME OF OLD-SCHOOL SELLING

over again. Recently, I was talking to one of my coaching clients about a prospect of his that he had gone through an entire sales cycle with, only to lose the deal in the end because the prospect decided to do the project in-house. My client had given him valuable information and free consulting—and he'd ended up with nothing in return.

Just the other day, the prospect called him up to ask for another proposal on a new project. My client was proud that, rather than jumping at the opportunity to do more free consulting, he brought the prospect through our Game Plan Selling system and got paid up-front for the proposal. Most salespeople would have jumped at the opportunity to be abused and cheated by the prospect all over again. Say this with me now, out loud: "No more!" You are an expert. Stop letting people treat you like anything but.

How it got this way

Now before you go and start a "Save the Salespeople" charity to protect them from the big bad prospect, let's explore how it became like this.

Imagine we took a walk into downtown Boston and asked a random sample of people to describe the average salesperson. The vast majority would describe the guy in this picture; that's just

Ready to buy from this guy?

the way salespeople are perceived. It's not one individual's fault, but rather a collective of experiences in the life of a prospect that's only further propagated by the media and popular culture.

If you ask a room full of people to describe what they associate with the word "salesperson," 100 out of 100 groups (even groups of salespeople—I've asked hundreds of times with zero variance) will collectively describe the worst salespeople they've ever met. This is what we're up against. It's nothing personal; it's just reality. The "profession" of selling, over the last century, has trained prospects to protect themselves from salespeople.

From now on, when you need to buy something, pay attention to how you behave when you go into "autopilot prospect mode." Chances are you'll instantly go to the Hide, Cheat and Steal system of buying.

For example, I recently went with a friend to help her buy a couch. When we entered the store, she was sure to walk as far away from the sales counter as possible to avoid the sales associates. Finally, when she had a question, she asked for some information from the sales associate. This salesperson was very high pressure and was doing everything he could to get her to buy the couch. After a while, he said to let him know if she wanted to get the couch. My friend politely said, "Of course." She then took some pictures of the couch with her iPhone along with the sales tag information.

We left the store and went home. When she got home, she went onto Google, entered in the information on the sales tag and bought the same couch from a different vendor for the same exact price. Hide, cheat and steal. In this particular case, the sale associate was exceptionally bad, but the point is that salespeople like him continue to perpetuate the negative image of our profession, and prospects know exactly how to respond.

How to Protect Yourself as a Salesperson

Whatever the prospect expects a salesperson to do, you should do the exact opposite. Think of it in terms of sports; if an opponent expects you to throw the football and you do, you are at a disadvantage. But if he expects you to throw and you run, then you have an advantage. The same goes for sales.

Rule #7: The solution to winning more sales is painfully simple: Be distinct.

Doing the unexpected will always benefit you. And in the case of sales, doing the unexpected is actually lower pressure and more authentic.

But in order to be distinct, you have to stop pitching, stop the enthusiasm, and stop persuading—"Stop the P.E.P!" Here's what I mean:

Stop Pitching: When a salesperson begins giving any type of presentation within the first half of a sales meeting, he is pitching. Jumping right into a pitch causes three bad things to happen:

1. The salesperson never takes the time to find out whether he's dealing with a prospect qualified for his services. In turn, the prospect isn't given the opportunity to reveal how and where he is hurting. As a result, the salesperson is diving into a sale without

the knowledge and understanding necessary to give the prospect what he needs and, therefore, close the sale.

2. By giving the pitch immediately, the salesperson is giving away valuable information right away—and for free. This makes both his services and his knowledge appear lower in value. I learned this lesson the hard way when I first began speaking professionally. In the beginning, I tried to give speeches for free to practice and gain experience. What I found was that no one wanted a free speech—no school, company or organization would accept the offer.

Rule #8: When you're a high-fee expert, clients treat you infinitely better than when you're begging to give your information away.

Once I had practiced enough and felt more confident, I approached the same kinds of groups—but this time, I was charging a fee. Instantly, business began to flow.

Since then, I've raised my speaking fee incrementally over time. And each time I raise my fee, I always worry that I will lose business because of the higher price. Instead, I've experienced the opposite. I now do business with organizations that wouldn't even have considered hiring me back when I charged less.

3. When a salesperson jumps into a pitch, it triggers the prospect's "anti-buying radar." You can actually *see* it happen.

For instance, last summer there was a church in downtown Boston looking for new members. A group of churchgoers set up shop on the corner of a busy intersection, smiling and handing out free granola bars to passersby. Since I believe you can learn a lot from your surroundings, I was fascinated to watch their strategy play out. Time after time, the same thing would happen: a member of the church would give a granola bar to a passerby, and the passerby would smile and keep on walking.

As passersby began to walk away with their granola bars, the church members would try to draw them back by diving into a pitch about their church services. Instantly, the passersby would break eye contact and quicken their pace to get away. People want to escape the second they sense a pitch is coming.

Rule #9: Think of yourself as a doctor, rather than a salesperson.

Stop the Enthusiasm: Being excessively enthusiastic is disingenuous and off-putting to prospects. Imagine receiving a call from an unknown number and answering only to be immediately bombarded by a loud and incredibly enthusiastic voice on the line. "Hi, how are you today!?!?!?!"

What does your gut instinct tell you to do? Hang up. It's a salesperson, and you know it before he even tells you why he's calling. You don't even know what he wants and you're already hanging up the phone.

It's time to start being authentic in selling situations—aim to connect with prospects by being real. They have seen the enthusiasm act a million times.

By being real and aiming to understand your prospect, you come off as distinct from the majority of salespeople out there. Think of yourself as a doctor, rather than a salesperson.

Rule #10: You don't want to persuade everyone to buy from you; you want the right people to buy from you.

When you go to the doctor with a problem in your knee, the doctor doesn't say "Well, I have a solution for YOU! You are simply going to LOVE this fantastic arthroscopic surgery that we can offer. It is so great!"

A good doctor asks you where it hurts, what it feels like, and what you've been doing that might have caused the pain. Mirror the doctor-patient dynamic in your sales life: replace all of that enthusiasm with a genuine desire to understand where prospects hurt and determine whether you can help them.

ARE YOU _TOO_ ENTHUSIASTIC?

Stop Persuading: It would take me all day to count the number of books written on effective persuasion in the past half-century. If you go to Amazon.com and search for books about persuasion, over 5,000 titles come up. That alone should be evidence enough that this concept is over-wrought and passé.

It's time for salespeople to stop spending all of their energy persuading people to work with them instead of focusing on understanding prospects. Prospects know the game of persuasion inside out. And what's more, you don't even want to persuade everyone to buy from you. You want the right people to buy from you, and you can't identify the right prospects if you're focused on persuasion.

I recently went looking for condos in Boston. A friend referred me to a real estate broker — and within minutes, I knew she wasn't the right broker for me. But against my better judgment, I decided to go. I was silent for the next three hours; she spoke non-stop about how great the properties were for me. Not once did she ask me what I was looking for, or take a step back and say, "Tell me why you want to move. What would be your ideal place?"

It was the longest three hours of my life. By the end, I felt I would go far out of my way to find a different broker to help me buy a place that she had showed me. It was just too much persuasion.

Rule #11: Rather than persuade, identify where your prospect hurts.

Rather than persuade, identify where your prospect hurts and seek to determine if the hurt is serious enough to do something about.

CHAPTER 6

The Opening Play

In this part of the book, you'll learn to craft your "Opening Play." Just like a sports team executes a tactical play at the start of the game to set the stage for success, you will open your dialogue with prospects in a strategic way. Think of your Opening Play as your "What I Do" statement. Some sales trainers might call this an "elevator pitch" — but, as you might imagine, the word "pitch" makes me queasy. Others might refer to it as your "thirty-second commercial" — but calling it a commercial makes you sound phony, and this is all about being genuine.

To give you a better idea of what your Opening Play should sound like, I'll share mine.

Marc Wayshak's Opening Play:

"I'm a sales coach who works with both businesses and entrepreneurs to create a game plan for selling. My clients come to me when they're losing too many sales to low-cost competitors, hearing "We'll think it over" from too many prospects, or getting inconsistent results from their sales efforts. Do any of these challenges ring true to you?"

Let's Break Down My Opening Play:

You want them to know exactly what you call yourself or what type of company you represent right away.

Tell them the types of clients you work with up front.

"I'm a sales coach who works with both businesses and entrepreneurs to create a game plan for selling.

Notice: clients come to me.

A very brief explanation of what you do—very brief.

My clients come to me when they're losing too many sales to low-cost competitors, hearing "We'll think it over" from too many prospects, or getting inconsistent results from their sales efforts.

Engage the prospect to say what challenges he's facing.

Briefly list common challenges your clients face.

Do any of these challenges ring true to you?"

It's very simple. More important, it's different from what your prospects are used to. Now, it's your turn. Imagine you're meeting with a potential prospect and he asks you to explain what you do in less than thirty seconds. What would you say? Say it out loud right now, and don't go to the next page until you do it.

Did you do any of the following?

✓ List all of the features your product or service has

✓ Enumerate all the benefits your service offers

✓ Say that you help customers grow their businesses

✓ Describe your company using superlatives (the best, fastest, happiest, etc.)

If you did, then you just did what every other salesperson out there is doing. And, as you remember, you don't want to be perceived as like everyone else. So, what is the exact opposite of telling people all about your company, products and services? Tell people about the common challenges that you solve for clients.

You want to engage the prospect as quickly as possible. Note that if you're using your Opening Play with the CEO of a large company it will be different than if you're telling it to a start-up entrepreneur. But no matter your audience, the essence of the Opening Play remains the same.

Now that you have a better idea of what your Opening Play should be, take a few minutes to write yours down:

Your New Opening Play:

"I am a/My company is a _____

[your profession or type of company]

who/that works with _____

[type of clients you have]

to _____.

[very briefly on what you do]

My clients come to me when they:

_____

[challenge # 1]

_____

[challenge # 2]

_____

[challenge # 3]

Do any of these challenges ring true to you?"

Now you have an Opening Play to start a productive conversation with prospects and set you apart from your competition. Type this up and practice it. This will be your go-to statement whenever people ask you what you do.

Your Opening Play will also be useful when we go over prospecting calls in a later section of this book.

Your Opening Play is the first piece of your new selling system; there will be no more "making stuff up" when you're in a

Rule #12: There's no more "making stuff up" when you're in a selling situation. It's all about being systematic

selling situation. It's all about being systematic—and the next chapter will be your guide.

BE SYSTEMATIC

...for every aspect of selling.

CHAPTER 7

Be Systematic

One of the most common themes in the sales community is that selling is a game of intuition, enthusiasm and instinct. It sounds nice—like it's a profession that comes naturally and requires little effort or knowledge. This couldn't be further from the truth.

> ## Rule #13: People are no more born with the skills to sell than they are born with the skills to play golf.

Selling is not a skill you're born with or without. In fact, that's a negative misconception that undermines the real nature of the game.

People are no more born with the skills to sell than they are born with the skills to play golf—yes, some people have qualities that predispose them to being golfers or salespeople, but the actual skills must be learned. Every beginning golfer must learn how to swing a club a certain way in order to hit the ball properly; every salesperson must learn a system in order to close sales.

WHY WE NEED A SYSTEM

By being systematic during the selling process, you're better able to focus on what really matters—what's going on in the mind of the prospect. After developing the skills to sell, in much the same way you learn any other skill, you will no longer be worried about what to say or do next in a selling situation. Then, if something goes wrong, you can isolate what the issue was because you do the exact same thing every time.

Client Case Study:

One of my clients, Danny, is the owner of a successful Internet marketing company based in Boston. Once we began working together, he instantly loved the idea of Game Plan Selling because he was a phenomenal rugby player and appreciated the connection between sports and sales. This guy, on the field, was the most vicious and ferocious person I'd ever seen. That mentality also translated off the field in the game of selling, in terms of his willingness to do whatever it took to achieve his sales goals.

However, Danny — like many others who sell high-end consulting services — had this problem: he would give his prospects an informative presentation only to lose the sale when they ran off to do the work in-house or with a cheaper vendor.

During our initial meeting, he gave me an example that resonated with the challenges faced by most salespeople. A large company had approached him to do a major Internet marketing campaign. Since it was a huge opportunity, Danny spent days honing his pitch, and even hired a designer to create preliminary artwork for the project.

Immediately after the presentation, the prospect told him the presentation was "to die for." They told him how great he was. How incredible the artwork was. How impressed they were with his company. They told him they had to think about it and weigh their options, but they would schedule a follow-up call "over the next week or so."

Danny was psyched about how the meeting went. For three days he walked around on air, thinking of everything he was going to do once he made this sale — he would have to hire some new staff, he might buy that car he wanted, and everyone in the company would get a nice year-end bonus. It was an exciting time.

A week later, Danny sent an email to the prospect to set up the follow-up meeting they had agreed upon. A day went by with no response. Two days, no response. Finally on the third day, he called the prospect. Straight to voicemail – he left a message. No call back. The prospect had disappeared.

Danny was frustrated and angry. He regularly tried to get through to the prospect by phone or email over the next few months but never got any response. Then about six months later, he saw that they had gone forward with his campaign – only without him. They had taken all of the ideas from his presentation and

Rule #14: There is no room in sales for improvisation.

used them. He was livid. He even considered suing them for stealing his ideas, but in the end he knew it was his own fault.

Danny had no system for selling, so he deferred to the prospect's system of buying – Hide, Cheat and Steal.

Thanks to experiences like this, Danny quickly implemented the Game Plan Selling system so that he could forever avoid being taken advantage of by prospects. There is no room in sales for improvisation. Everything must be part of your game plan in selling.

This next section of the book is about creating that end-to-end game plan: from the first conversation, to face-to-face sales meetings, to prospecting calls.

The Game Plan: Connect, Disqualify, Case Study

This three-step selling system lays out what you must do throughout every phase of a sale so that you will never have to improvise again. One central tenet of Game Plan Selling is that you must have a script for every aspect of selling. You want to know your lines so that way you don't have to think about it when you are actually in the selling situation. The three parts to the Game Plan are:

Connect: Sales trainers always talk about establishing rapport with prospects. That's all well and good, but a deeper connection with prospects is needed to ultimately close sales.

Rule #15: Every prospect expects to be qualified; no prospect wants to be disqualified.

Disqualify: If a prospect doesn't hurt in his current or future situation, then he is not qualified for your services. Your goal is to disqualify the prospect. Every prospect expects to be qualified; no prospect wants to be disqualified.

Case Study Presentation: Most salespeople start with a presentation. In Game Plan Selling, the presentation comes last. Furthermore, all presentations are kept to a minimum, consisting of examples and case studies rather than the features and benefits of your services.

CHAPTER 8

Connect

As I mentioned earlier, most sales literature recommends establishing rapport with prospects. Rapport is defined in the Merriam Webster Dictionary as "relation marked by affinity." This is a positive thing — you want the prospect to have a good feeling about you. But it's also incomplete.

> **Rule #16: People don't buy from people they like; they buy from people who understand them.**

I have had clients pay me very large sums of money even though we had nothing in common personally. They just believed that I understood their challenges and knew that I could help solve them.

To be clear, I'm not suggesting that you shouldn't talk about the Red Sox if you and your prospect are both big Red Sox fans. I'm merely suggesting that such a connection alone isn't substantial enough to build a successful sales relationship.

Let me give you an example. I'm a big fan of the New England Patriots (probably not surprising since I'm from Boston). A few years back, I had to get health insurance through a provider since I was self-employed. An agent came over to my place and we sat down. He saw the New England Patriots plaque that I had up on my wall and for the next two minutes we bonded over our mutual love for the Pats.

After that, I had a good feeling about him—but that's all it was. Then, for the next twenty minutes, he enthusiastically told me everything that I needed to know about insurance, never once asking me what my priorities were. In the end, I said I'd think about it. Later that day, I decided to go with a different agent. He just didn't take the time to understand my situation and so I felt no connection to him, despite our common interests.

Establishing a Connection

The two components to establishing a connection are:

1. Be perceived as similar to the prospect: You want prospects to feel you're similar to them—not necessarily in terms of having things in common, but in terms of how you relate to their situation. This can be achieved by matching and mirroring prospects during phone and in-person meetings.

2. Be authentic by seeking to understand: If the prospect perceives you as "salesy," then he will shut down and no connection will be established. People only open up to those that understand them. A connection with a prospect is ultimately created when he senses that you're seeking to understand his situation.

Note that you must have both components in alignment in order to establish a connection with a prospect. One of the two is nice, but it's not a connection.

Be Perceived as Similar

Let me ask you a question—who is your favorite person in the world? If you're going through a list of people you know, just stop right there, you're already off track.

Your favorite person is you. Your prospect's favorite person is himself. It's just the way people are wired. That's how we've survived for the millions of years we've existed as a species. At the end of the day, we must like ourselves more than anyone else in order to survive the evolutionary process.

Therefore, if the prospect believes that you're similar to him, he will begin to feel connected to you. In order to be perceived as similar to your prospect, you must match and mirror him.

Matching and mirroring is all about thinking of yourself as a chameleon. While you don't want to seem fake, you do want to adapt to your surroundings. There are three key aspects of your prospect you want to mirror called the Three V's:

Visual: How he looks, moves and carries himself

Voice: The tone and pace of his voice

Vibe: His mood and presence

It's your job to be perceived as similar to your prospect on all three of these fronts.

Visual: One of the most important things to remember is this: dress like your prospects. Most sales trainers will tell you to dress to impress. Dressing to impress may actually hurt your chances of closing a sale. Imagine that we've filled a room with

---

Rule #17: Most sales trainers will tell you to dress to impress. Dressing to impress may actually hurt your chances of closing a sale.

Silicon Valley startup entrepreneurs mostly in their mid to late twenties. They're wearing T-shirts, jeans and sandals. And it's your job to get them to buy your product or service.

Would wearing a three-piece Armani suit with pointy-toed shoes and a flashy ring endear you to that group of prospects? Heck no. They will instantly shut down when they see you, even before they hear all the great things you have to offer them. It's over before it even begins.

ARE YOU BREAKING CONNECTION WITH YOUR PROSPECTS?

On the other hand, if I told you to sell your product or service to a room full of New Jersey nightclub owners, that fancy outfit may be a perfect match. Dress like your prospects. I see young salespeople dressing in high-end, fashionable clothes all the time—even though they sell to predominantly middle-aged men. That mismatch is costing them major sales.

Voice: In terms of matching the tone and pace of a prospect's voice, it's important to listen carefully to how he sounds. If your prospect is quiet and slow-paced, change your voice to sound similar. If the prospect, on the other hand, is loud and booming with a fast pace, then match your voice accordingly.

Vibe: Likewise, mirror your prospect's mood and presence by paying attention to body language. If your prospect appears shy and slow-moving, ease up on eye contact and slow down your movements. This component of matching and mirroring also covers the hand shake. Many sales trainers teach their clients to always have a strong handshake. This is a mistake. If your prospect's grip is on the weaker side, loosen yours. On the other hand, if your prospect has a very strong grip, then have at it and show off your strong grip.

It's all about matching and mirroring the three V's — visual, vocal and vibe.

Be Authentic by Seeking to Understand

> # Rule #18: Match the "right you" to the prospect.

I know that some people reading this are thinking to themselves, "He just told me to be a chameleon and *now* he wants me to be authentic?" That's exactly right. These two concepts are not at odds with each other, although it might seem that way. Stop thinking of yourself as a static personality.

Humans have dynamic personalities, meaning that you don't have just one personality. You have many personalities, depending upon your mood, the environment and necessity.

The key to establishing a connection with a prospect is to match the "right you" to the prospect on a visual, vocal and vibe level.

In short, don't go into enthusiastic and persuasive sales-person mode. I have never experienced it, but I could imagine that if I were to sell, for example, extreme sports travel tours (where you travel around the world with a group of like-minded thrill-seeking people and experience extreme sport after extreme sport) then yes, I might get very enthusiastic during a selling situation. Aside from rare situations like that, the excessive enthusiasm should be left at the door.

In almost every case, being enthusiastic will be perceived as being "salesy," and the prospect will shut down. Just be real and aim to understand his situation.

Make the purpose of every interaction with prospects about them and their specific needs. Ask questions that explore where the prospect hurts.

There will be much more on the specifics of how to do this as we continue going through the Game Plan Selling system. Right now, the key is to change your mindset. In both my audio courses and live trainings, I take you through a number of exercises to help you shift your focus toward a prospect-centered perspective. However, since we can't do that in a book, it's time to simply practice matching and mirroring immediately. Practice with friends, family and prospects.

CHAPTER 9

Disqualify

There is a wide range of reasons why a prospect isn't a fit for you. Whatever the reason, it's your job to discover if a prospect isn't a fit as quickly as possible. You're no longer in the business of convincing people to buy your stuff; you're in the business of identifying who does and does not need your stuff.

> ## Rule #19: Realistically, at least fifty percent of your prospects will not be a good fit for your services.

As I've said before, when I first began selling I was taught that I should just give the most persuasive presentation that I possibly could. After about a year of using this old-school technique, I began bringing the same PowerPoint presentation with me to each meeting. It was really nice. I learned how to make fancy graphics with moving objects on the screen and I would list off all of the benefits that the prospect would enjoy by working with me.

I had my presentation down to a science. I had practiced it hundreds of times in front of a mirror and in front of my family — who, by the way, was very impressed by it. This thing was tight.

Yet when I'd go out to meet with prospects to show them all the incredible benefits I had to offer them, they would inevitably say something like, "This is really impressive. Let me think it over and we can go from there."

Proud of myself for giving a flawless presentation, I would go buy myself a big steak dinner to celebrate the impending sale.

Rule #20: Great salespeople do not get compliments from prospects; they get orders.

In almost every case, though, the sale never happened. There were a few that closed, but most of the time I got lost in the follow-up phase. Looking back, I don't know how I was able to lie to myself so effectively about being a great salesman. I now know that great salespeople do not get compliments from prospects; they get orders.

But back then, I just didn't know. Always stuck in the follow-up phase, I had a constant list of about fifty prospects I would call a few times per month. Each time, nothing had changed. My biggest fear was that they would say that they'd decided not to work with me. I was trying to avoid a "no."

In 2008, the New England Patriots went into the Super Bowl with a perfect record. Many critics and fans agreed that this was likely the greatest football team ever. Yet on February 3rd 2008, the New England Patriots lost in a close game to the New York Giants. All of that praise was meaningless in the end because the Patriots simply didn't finish the job.

Salespeople tell me all the time about how close they are to closing a deal or what a great job they've done in a sales meeting—it's all wasted breath. What matters is whether the prospect gives you a check that doesn't bounce.

Rule #21: Ninety percent of what's in a salesperson's pipeline is pure junk.

Old-school selling prescribes doing everything in one's power to avoid the dreaded "no." So what happens is that sales-people spend half of their time just following up on prospects stuck in their pipelines.

Think about your current pipeline of prospects right now. Let's pretend you hired me to call those prospects and say the following:

"Hello [Prospect's Name], my name is Marc Wayshak and I'm looking for feedback on your connection with [Your Name]. Please be brutally honest. Do you have any intention of working with [Your Name]?"

My guess is that most of the prospects in your current pipeline would tell me they have no intention of working with you. But, people hate confrontation, so they lead us on. It's a terrible waste of everyone's time, but it's not the prospects fault.

Rule #22: People hate a sales pitch, but they love buying stuff.

Salespeople, by trying to get prospects to tell them "yes," set themselves up to waste time with prospects who never intended to work with them in the first place but were too "nice" to just say "no." There is an old truism in sales that goes like this: "People hate a sales pitch, but they love buying stuff."

We all love to buy. I could spend hours in stores like Best Buy, Home Depot or Target. I love buying all sorts of things, but the second I believe that I'm being sold, I don't enjoy it anymore.

By making it a goal to disqualify prospects, suddenly your pipeline consists of only viable potential clients. And it shrinks dramatically.

This gives you much more time to focus on finding new prospects, whether it's by finishing that marketing campaign you've been putting off, making more prospecting calls or asking current clients for introductions.

What was most liberating to me when I finally adopted Game Plan Selling into my professional life was that I suddenly had more time to get productive things done. Now that I wasn't spending half of my time "following up," I could focus on what really mattered—finding good prospects, closing deals, and then actually enjoying a social life.

That's why you must change your goals when it comes to prospects. Your goal from now on is to *disqualify* prospects. This works on the concept of reverse psychology: prospects *expect* you to qualify them, and they *don't want* you to disqualify them.

Rule #23: Hurt you can solve + money to invest = qualified prospect.

It goes back to that doctor's mindset. A good doctor will thoroughly examine a patient before telling the patient if there is a solution to the problem. Only a quack will offer a solution without identifying and exploring the real problem first. We must have this same mindset with our prospects. That means that after you have connected with a prospect, it's time to disqualify.

To help you do this successfully, let's first outline the differences between an unqualified prospect and a qualified prospect. An unqualified prospect has interest; a qualified prospect is hurting. The goal of Game Plan Selling is to disqualify all prospects who aren't hurting about their current or likely future situation.

I recently worked with a large mortgage company in the western part of the U.S., and they were really hurting very badly over their current situation.

The salespeople simply weren't prospecting efficiently, so they weren't hitting their numbers. They were losing talent left and right to a tough market. And the CEO was worried he might lose his job over the lack of performance. He still had two kids in college and needed to save his job to pay the bills. When we met, I was able to identify a lot of hurt right away.

I also recently worked with a small tech startup with a three-person sales team. The salespeople were all in their twenties and had no process for selling. They were going around giving presentations to prospects, but they weren't closing any sales.

What was interesting about this company was that it was very well-funded by venture capitalists, and they already had one very large client. So the company did not actually have a lot of hurt about their current financial situation. Nonetheless, the company's CEO was very worried about the future.

In a newly developing market, there was a battle raging between three companies to become "the standard." Once a standard is established, the other two competitors will become second and third choices for prospects. This means that the company was in a fight for its life. So an ineffective sales team didn't cause them financial hurt at the moment, but future hurt would be massive unless they developed their salespeople into top performers.

The CEO had made this company his life's passion. If he failed, he explained to me, he would be devastated.

Hurt over a current situation or a possible future situation makes for qualified prospects — as long as they also have the money to pay you. Anything less means you're dealing with an unqualified prospect you need to disqualify.

For some strange reason, the quest to find a prospect's hurt is controversial. Many sales trainers argue that you don't need to find the hurt, but rather just help the prospect see how much he will gain by working with you. That is simply faux-science, and I can prove it with a simple experiment.

(Note: Do not try this at home.)

Imagine that you're holding both hands out in front of you with your palms down. Underneath one hand, there's a stack of $10,000 in cash. Underneath the other hand, there's a very hot flame. You can only move one hand. Which do you move?

The reality is that any sane person will move away from the hot flame rather than grab the $10,000. Human beings will go much further to avoid being hurt than to gain pleasure. Use this human instinct to your advantage.

CHAPTER 10

Disqualification Checklist

Your primary goal in selling from this day forth should be to disqualify those prospects who aren't hurting from a problem you can solve. You do this by asking a targeted series of questions. Prospects must be able to answer your questions such that they prove themselves to be qualified.

Thus, after you have connected with a prospect, begin the conversation by taking the prospect through the Disqualification Checklist:

✓ Does the prospect have challenges you solve?	Yes
✓ Has the prospect fixed the problems yet?	No
✓ Do the problems cost a significant amount?	Yes
✓ Is the prospect personally affected?	Yes
✓ Is he willing to invest enough money in a solution?	Yes
✓ Can he make the decision?	+ Yes

√ Qualified

From now on, whenever you're in a selling situation, you want to identify these six points. To be clear, these aren't the actual questions you would ask the prospect, as they're all close-ended questions and will not lead to discussion. Your goal is to have the prospect paint you a picture of these six points by asking him open-ended questions, which I will share with you shortly.

This checklist is simply for your purposes, to identify whether the prospect is qualified. If you don't get the right answer to any of these questions, then your prospect is not currently qualified and you want to move on as quickly as possible to focus on prospects who are qualified.

Rule #24: Know what challenges you solve and only help people with those particular challenges.

The Checklist Point By Point:

1. Does the prospect have challenges you can solve? In my world, the kind of hurt I can solve revolves around the ability to bring in top-line revenue. I help salespeople, companies and entrepreneurs increase their sales. I don't help companies improve their operations. If prospects are hurting badly over assembly line issues, I'm not their guy.

If a prospect is not hurting over something I can fix, then that person is not qualified to work with me. Period. And the same goes for you. Know what challenges you solve and only help people with those particular challenges.

Here are some conversation starters that will help you identify whether the prospect is qualified for your help:

1. "Tell me about your challenges with regards to…"

2. "Give me an example of that challenge."

3. "Tell me a little more about the biggest challenges you face."

2. Has the prospect already fixed his problems? This may sound like an obvious point, but I've had prospects tell me all about their challenges and completely forget to tell me that they have a plan in place working to solve those problems. If a prospect is in the middle of implementing a seemingly effective program that will solve his problems, then he is likely not a fit yet.

On the other hand, if he hasn't tried to fix his problems, it's a good indicator that he may not be hurting much. For example, the computer I'm using to write this book is two years old and making funny noises. I have software that backs up my entire hard drive in the event that the computer dies.

Nonetheless, one of my challenges is that this computer is making funny noises and distracting me. Have I done anything to fix the problem? No. Am I hurting enough to motivate me to buy a new computer? No. I have a challenge, but the hurt isn't deep enough to motivate me to action. I haven't done anything to try to fix it because I simply don't care enough.

Here are some questions you can ask to help you identify whether the prospect qualifies for your help:

1. "What have you done to fix your problem?"

2. "How's that working?"

3. "Why haven't you done anything to fix your problem?"

3. Do the problems cost him a significant amount of money? If a challenge is costing a major pharmaceutical firm only $1 million in sales, it probably isn't worth doing anything about.

Rule #25: Identify what the challenges are costing a prospect in actual dollars.

However, if a challenge is costing a small landscape company $1 million, that's probably a pivotal amount of money being left on the table or lost. The goal here is to identify what the challenges are costing a prospect or company in actual dollars.

Exception: There are some people reading this book who sell products or services to which dollars lost may not be relevant. That's okay. I had a coaching client who sold high-end cabinets to homeowners. I never realized how much people spend on cabinets until I met this client. His average sale was easily fifty thousand dollars.

When he would take people through the Game Plan Selling system, he would tailor his questions to find out what clients felt they were losing out on by having outdated or unappealing cabinetry. Some would say it was hurting the value of their home and give a dollar amount. Others would tell him they lacked enough storage space in the kitchen, or they were just unhappy with the appearance of their home. Either way, my client was able to pinpoint exactly what the problem of unsatisfactory cabinetry was "costing" his prospects.

If, like many salespeople, you sell your products or services to businesses, then accept nothing short of a dollar estimate of what the problem costs the prospect. Here are some questions you can ask to help you identify whether the prospect qualifies for your help:

1. "What does this problem cost you?"

2. "How much would you estimate that this problem costs you?"

3. "Can you ball park what this costs you?"

4. Is he personally affected by the problems? Salespeople love to assume that just because someone has a professional challenge, a prospect wants to spend the time and money to fix it. This

---

Rule #26: If a prospect isn't hurting personally due to a problem, he won't put in the effort to resolve it.

---

couldn't be further from the truth. When push comes to shove, people won't do anything to change a situation unless it affects them personally. If a prospect isn't hurting personally due to a problem, he won't put in the effort to resolve it.

If a prospect needs to solve his sales problems in order to pay for his daughter's college tuition, he's personally affected by his company's challenges. He's hurting if he's spending ninety hours a week chasing leads.

Here are some questions you can ask to help identify whether the prospect qualifies for your help:

1. "How does this problem affect you personally?"

2. "Why is solving this problem important to you?"

3. "Why are you committed to finding a solution?"

5. Is he willing to invest enough money in a solution? You know who needs your product or service more than anybody? The person who can't afford it. Broke people are hurting more than anyone out there, but they simply don't have the money to do anything about it. I once had a prospect who owned a company in the pay phone business. Crying in front of me because she needed my help so badly, she was willing to do whatever it took to solve her challenges. The only problem was that she had no money. She was flat broke.

Rule #27: The person who needs your product or service the most is the one who can't afford it.

I felt awful, but there was really nothing I could do. I gave her my first book as a gift and wished her the best of luck. She ultimately closed shop and found a different job. I have a right to be paid for my services and so do you.

Prospects will ultimately resent you for giving them your stuff for free. Don't do it. Rather, spend your time finding prospects with both enough hurt and enough money to be able to *invest* in your product or service. There is tremendous value in what you sell; you must be paid accordingly for it.

Rule #28: It's time to start asking about the prospect's budget.

The prospect doesn't have the right to demand you tell him what your product or service costs. You have the right to know what the prospect's budget is first. If you walked away from this book taking only one piece of advice, I would want it to be that you begin asking prospects for a budget early on in deliberations.

I have a client who sells high-end landscape construction services. When I first started working with his company, the landscape architects were simply giving a quote for what their work would cost. This is ludicrous. How can you give a quote on something that can range so greatly in cost? When I asked, he told me that a typical project could range anywhere from twenty thousand to five-hundred thousand dollars.

Immediately, we changed their selling process to ask prospects for their budgets.

Here are some questions you can ask to help you identify whether the prospect qualifies for your help:

1. "Do you have a budget to solve your issues?"

2. "What's your budget?"

3. "How much could you imagine investing to fix your problems?"

Note: Don't assume that the first number a prospect tells you is his maximum budget; simply take it as an indicator of what a prospect is willing to invest. Once you have that initial number, you can start to test the limit.

6. Is he ready to make a decision? Have you ever done a great job with a prospect who was hurting, really wanted your services, had the money, but turned out not to be the decision maker? If you've been in sales for any length of time, then you've had this frustrating experience.

Rule #29: Avoid giving presentations to non-decision makers.

One of my clients who sells real estate would always tell me about the husband and wife dynamic in his world. He told me that for his entire career selling real estate — until he adopted the Game Plan Selling system — he lost sales because he wasn't dealing with the real decision maker. He said that the most common scenario would be a husband acting like he called the shots, when in reality the wife had the final word.

The key is to avoid giving presentations to non-decision makers unless absolutely necessary. Most often, these people only have the power to say "no;" they don't have the power to say "yes." Always press to have all key decision-makers present before you present any type of solution.

Here are some questions you can ask to help you identify whether the prospect qualifies for your help:

1. "Who else is involved in making this decision?"

2. "Is there anyone else that we need to include in this conversation before we move forward?

3. "What is your decision-making process for this project?"

The goal in the disqualification phase of Game Plan Selling is to ensure that you are dealing with a fully qualified prospect. Be sure to ask questions that confirm each component of the Disqualification Checklist.

Now it's time to learn one of the most powerful tools in the Disqualify phase — the Swim Move.

CHAPTER 11

The Swim Move

The **Swim Move:** Use prospects' own "force" — their questions and statements — to learn more about them and keep control of a sale.

When I played football, I was a linebacker on defense. My favorite play was blitzing the quarterback in an attempt to sack or tackle him. It was exhilarating because I had to break through the offensive line in order to make the play.

There are two ways to break through the line. The first way is to go head-to-head with a lineman and overpower him to break through. This is extremely difficult — especially because most linemen are bigger than I am.

The second way — which became my go-to move — is to break through the line by using what's called the "swim move." In a well-performed swim move, I would use the offensive lineman's own force against him.

Let me explain. The lineman's goal is to keep me away from the quarterback. My goal is to get past the lineman, whose strategy is most likely going to involve pushing me back. His strength is his ability to push forward; but that's also his weakness. Since I know that the lineman is going to try to push me back, I let him do so—but I also move to the side. As long as I've moved out of the way, he'll push through at nothing. I've just used his own force and energy against him. The swim move, when done effectively, is incredibly powerful. Now, how does it apply to sales?

Prospects have been conditioned—both by experience and society—to assume the worst in salespeople. As part of their defense mechanism against the typical salesman, prospects will ask leading questions and make certain statements aimed at "disqualifying" salespeople.

Rule #30: A prospect does everything for a reason, and you can never assume you know what that reason is.

But Game Plan Selling is all about turning the old-school prospect-salesperson dynamic on its head. So instead of letting prospects use the power of their questions and statements to disqualify you, you're going to learn how to leverage what they say to either close the sale or make a disqualification of your own.

DO YOU ASSUME YOU KNOW WHAT YOUR PROSPECTS WANT?

When it comes to the Disqualify phase of Game Plan Selling, your ultimate goal is to dig as deeply as possible in your quest to understand where and how badly the prospect hurts. Throughout this process, prospects will make statements or ask questions. These aren't just conversation pieces—they're clues that need to be uncovered in order to be useful to you.

A prospect says and does everything for a reason, and you can never assume you know what that reason is. That's why it's important never to assume you know how to respond to something a prospect does or says. Instead, before answering, you have to do some "research" by way of some questions and statements of your own.

Imagine, for example, that a prospect asks you, "Do you work with any other clients in my industry?"

Your instinct might tell you to answer immediately, and probably in the affirmative, to show the prospect that you have relevant experience and knowledge. However, there might be more to his question than you think.

He might, as you suspect, want to do business with a company that knows his industry well. But, on the other hand, he might want to do business with someone who has no other clients in his industry to avoid a conflict of interest. Or, if you work with his number-one competitor, he might not want to work with you. Game over.

The salesperson who immediately answers that question in the affirmative ends his chance of doing business with the client.

Instead, imagine if the prospect asks, "Do you work with any other clients in my industry?" and the salesperson responds with a noncommittal, "Great question. Why do you ask?"

A possible response is, "Well, I don't want to work with someone who already works with our competitors."

If the salesperson doesn't work with the prospect's competitors, then he can say so. If, however, he does work with the prospect's competitors, he can respond with a question such as, "Is that a deal breaker?" If the prospect says "yes," then the salesperson has at least saved himself time and effort—he knows right away the prospect isn't a fit.

No matter the prospect's answer, the salesperson is automatically armed with more information than he had before.

While continuing the quest for more knowledge about a prospect, a salesperson often hears a statement like, "I worked with your competitor and it was a disaster." Most salespeople would simply agree, saying, "Yeah, we've heard bad things." But if you're in the habit of knocking your competition—which many salespeople are—you're hurting your credibility and failing to leverage the prospect's statement for your advantage.

Rule #31: Always answer a question with a question.

In the view of Game Plan Selling, a prospect's negative remark about the salesperson's competitor is a golden opportunity to discover more about the prospect's hurt. All the salesperson has to say is, "What do you mean by that? Tell me what happened."

Follow this through throughout the sales process: always answer a question with a question.

By using your swim move, you use the prospect's own words to create an opportunity. Here are some examples of what an effective swim move might sound like:

- ➤ "Why do you ask?"

- ➤ "Interesting. What do you mean by that?"

- ➤ "Help me understand."

- ➤ "Great question. You must be asking for a reason."

All four of those swim moves are inviting the prospect to clarify why he said or asked something. This allows the prospect to do all of the heavy lifting for you.

This technique is hard to use at first for one simple reason: we have been trained our entire lives to answer questions we are asked. Literally since pre-school you've received accolades for answering a question correctly.

Rule #32: It's not your job to read minds. Just ask.

The only problem is that when we jump to answer questions right away, we miss huge opportunities to gain valuable information from the prospect.

Plus, if our only job as salespeople was to answer questions, then we'd be obsolete. Who would need a salesperson in the days of Google? It's time to undo that learning and practice your swim move with friends and family. Just don't tell them that you're doing it—they won't notice.

If you've ever been to a psychologist, then you've seen this technique in action. Ask a psychologist something like, "Do you think I should quit my job?" The psychologist will respond, "Why do you ask? Do *you* think you should quit your job?"

They've been trained to do this in order to understand the deeper meaning behind patients' statements and questions. Begin by practicing this in low-risk situations—like at home or out at dinner with friends—and then work your way up to selling situations.

Now that you're disqualifying, you can relax during a sale. It's not an arm wrestling match of wills. It's a dialogue, led by you through questioning. And through the flow of conversation, the qualified prospect uncovers that he needs what you have. By the end of a proper Disqualification conversation, a prospect will be eager to see how you can help him.

CHAPTER 12

Case Study Presentation

Old-school sales trainers all teach a variation of "feature and benefit" selling. They'll tell you to describe your product or service as a series of features that will provide benefits to prospects.

Walking into a prospect's office and listing off the benefits of your services is like saying, "I'm just like every other salesperson out there."

Rule #33: Almost all salespeople are using the "feature and benefit" selling technique. Stop.

I used to be the king of feature and benefit selling. A sales trainer once taught me to draw a line down the middle of a sheet of paper, writing all of the features of my services on the left and all of their benefits on the right. That piece of paper was my entire focus during a sales call. I thought I was cutting-edge, but I soon realized that everyone else was doing the same exact thing.

This is the problem with sales techniques in general. A new technique comes along and it works really well. As a result, sales trainers start teaching that technique to all of their clients. Suddenly, everyone is using the same technique. Prospects start to see a pattern, and eventually the technique stops working.

The good news is that it takes many decades for a new sales technique to become commonplace.

> # Rule #34: You and your services will immediately seem higher-value to the prospect when you ask them good, meaningful questions.

The first core principle of Game Plan Selling is to be distinct from your prospects. The way to do that in a presentation is two-fold.

First, make your presentation the last part of your sales meeting. By having a meaningful thirty- to sixty-minute conversation about the prospect's business or situation *before* giving your presentation, you will automatically set yourself apart from other salespeople. Prospects expect you to rush through a few "probing questions" and then get right to your pitch. You and your services will immediately seem higher-value to the prospect when you take the time to ask good, meaningful questions.

Second, give as short a presentation as possible. That presentation should be based predominantly on case studies—real-life examples of comparable sales situations and their outcomes. Examples are infinitely more powerful than lists of the features and benefits of your product or service. Not only do case studies make it easier for prospects to grasp what you can do to help them, they also make your presentation much more interesting.

Just think back to your high school history class. Did you ever learn about the thirteenth-century English king, Edward I, and how he treated the Scottish people? Even if you did, you probably forget by now. But if you've ever seen the movie "Braveheart," there's no doubt that you remember what the British did to the Scottish in the thirteenth century.

If teachers really want their students to learn about a particular time in history, they should show them documentaries or movies, or give them witnesses' first-hand accounts and historical fiction to read. It's much easier—and more exciting—to have a conversation about a well-told story or the life of a relatable person than it is to discuss dry facts. The same concept applies to sales presentations.

How to Use the Case Study Presentation

It's your job to be ready to present a case study or two based on the type of hurt your prospect has. I will share two case studies that I regularly use.

Rule #35: Have a repertoire of case studies that appeal to prospect's hurt.

One type of client I deal with quite regularly is a mid-sized ($3 to $50 million) company with sales teams ranging from five to fifty salespeople. The most common types of hurt these clients suffer from are the following:

> Prospecting techniques that once worked are no longer working,

> The sales team has a decent pipeline but isn't closing a lot of deals, and

> There aren't a lot of "A" players on the sales team — in other words, the top 20% of salespeople outsell the other 80%.

I'm always prepared with case studies exemplifying each of these three types of hurt. After I've connected and decided not to disqualify the prospect, I'll give the prospect a brief presentation of case studies based on the type of hurt exhibited.

One Case Study That I Would Use:

One client that had these same issues mentioned was a bank that I worked with. The bank had twenty-five salespeople with a range of titles — from vice president to customer service representative. Money was getting tight. Any prospecting techniques that had worked during the years of high liquidity no longer worked.

The salespeople were stuck chasing the same fruitless leads they had in the past. There were three star salespeople on the team; the rest were "B" and "C" players.

This client of mine needed to appeal to more up-market companies in order to lend capital — and avoid bankruptcy.

When I began working with the bank, the first thing I did was assess its existing sales team. I looked for its strengths and its weaknesses. After discerning what needed to be improved upon, I worked with the entire sales team in three-hour segments every two weeks. I taught everyone a uniform selling system so they could all speak the same language and identify where and when problems were taking place.

This was the start of a total sales culture transformation.

The salespeople began to monitor their daily prospecting activities. After two weeks of compiling that data, I brought them together to pool their information. Based on what we discovered about their prospecting habits, we worked together to create a sale-generating plan for daily prospecting — the Prospecting Playbook.

Next on the agenda was a new hiring process. The bank needed more "A" players, and I suspected their existing hiring process was a roadblock. The management had a very informal hiring process based on the "feeling" they got about job candidates. Together we revamped the system. The new hiring process consisted of a scripted phone interview, followed by a rigorous online assessment to determine candidates' sales qualifications and relevant knowledge. If candidates did well enough, they then entered into a series of interviews designed to simulate selling situations common to the banking industry.

Within three months of instituting its personalized Game Plan Selling system, my client had hired five strong salespeople. The existing sales team was spending its time on prospecting activities that actually led to sales. Morale was higher than it had been in years because the team had a clear plan for success. And, most important, commercial sales (with a mix of lending and services) had increased across the board.

Another Case Study That I Would Use:

Another type of client that I commonly work with in my Platinum Coaching Program is an entrepreneur with revenues of between $250,000 and $5 million. This person is often the key salesperson along with many other responsibilities. An entrepreneur in this position commonly deals with the following challenges:

➢ Responsibility for multiple business functions which makes it difficult to sell consistently,

➢ Lack of prospects in pipeline,

➢ Receiving "I'll think it over's" from prospects, and

➢ Unexplained lack of company growth over periods of months or years.

For a prospect in this position, I might share the story of a past client of mine with a relevant hurt—Bill, an entrepreneur who started his own screen printing company.

Bill founded the company in his late twenties. Thanks to some large corporate clients, business grew quickly and steadily for about fifteen years. His sales were up around $5 million by the time I met him. He had built a comfortable life for his family, but recently his industry had changed. Clients were price-checking him against large, online vendors, many of which were overseas. Sales had begun to slump and margins tightened.

Bill had never really thought of himself as a salesperson. With the exception of having to attend the occasional client lunch or presentation, sales generally rolled in on their own. But now that had changed. Bill suddenly had to generate sales or he was going to have to lay off employees who had been with him for over a decade. He would have to cut back on personal expenses — maybe even sell his home.

The problem was that Bill simply didn't know where to start.

He had hired a telemarketer, but that didn't work. Then he tried a direct-mail campaign, but got no responses. He even tried to stop in on some large companies nearby, but he never got past the receptionist.

When Bill joined my Game Plan Selling Platinum Coaching program, the first thing I did was get him up to speed on the Game Plan Selling system. I taught him how to be distinct from the competition — and how to use the three steps of the Game Plan.

Bill immediately loved the idea of building connections with prospects. He knew he was good at building rapport—mostly by talking about the Red Sox or Celtics—but he had never thought about going beyond that. He began matching and mirroring his prospects, and he made sure his sales calls were focused

---

Rule #36: It's not about price; it's about rescuing clients from their hurt.

---

on his prospects' issues and challenges, not his services and products.

He explained how this technique immediately took pressure off of him. He used to hate "tap dancing in front of a client," as he put it, and now he could just be genuine and get even more results.

Disqualifying prospects was a big change in mindset for Bill. Once he began using the script of questions to uncover prospects' hurt and identify whether they were qualified for his services, he was able to understand prospects on a much deeper level. Furthermore, he told me that he realized it wasn't just about price anymore; it was about how he was rescuing clients from their challenges.

After giving his first case study presentation, Bill noticed that his prospects were far more interested in what he had to say as they could really visualize what he would do for them.

Finally, I helped him develop his Prospecting Playbook, a compilation of prospecting activities that he could track and perform on a daily basis to generate sales leads.

Within six months of working together, Bill landed a deal with a major corporate client as its sole provider of screen-printing—a contract worth $200,000 per year—as well as a few new mid-sized clients. He explained how these new clients treated him differently from his old clients because they saw him as a partner and marketing resource rather the just a "T-shirt guy."

Rule #37: Keep your presentations short and sweet.

Remember, once you're presenting to a prospect, you're at your most vulnerable. You're no longer in the position to disqualify a prospect; you've tacitly acknowledged that you think he's a fit by presenting about your service or product.

With this in mind, it's important to focus on two things in particular. The first, like I said earlier, is that you want to keep the presentation as short as possible. Don't go any longer than you have to.

The second point is that you want to let the prospect interrupt you during the presentation. If the prospect so much as looks like he's about to say something, stop and ask, "Did you have a question about that?" If the prospect asks you a question, use your swim move.

By encouraging questions and comments during your presentation, you're keeping it collaborative.

After you've completed your presentation, it's time for your big closing statement. Except it's not a statement—it's actually a question: "What would you like to do next?"

If the prospect is ready to move forward then he will let you know. On the other hand, he may tell you that this is not the right solution. However, if you did a thorough job in the disqualification phase, then this is an unlikely outcome. If the prospect is

---

Rule #38: Always close with the question: "What would you like to do next?"

---

not ready to move forward, he will more likely tell you that he needs to 'think this over.' If the prospect tells you that he wants to think it over, do not take this statement at face value. He may simply need some more help getting to the close.

This is the part where you want to say what you are thinking. If you think that the prospect is trying to tell you 'no' but wants to be nice, then say so. Gently tell the prospect that it sounds like he doesn't want your product or service. If you have done a thorough job up until now, he will push back at you and say that's not the case. This is where your swim move comes into play again. Ask, "What do you mean when you say that's not the case?" He will explain. In the event that a prospect cannot make a decision in that particular meeting, be sure to schedule a next step while you are still face-to-face. Don't allow for vague next steps, you want to schedule something solid.

Rule #39: If you were strong in the beginning, the end is the easiest part of the meeting.

Note: I don't spend a lot of time on this part of the sale because the most important part of the meeting is the beginning. If you're getting tremendous pushback towards the end of a meeting, it's probably because you didn't effectively disqualify or identify where the prospect hurts.

This is the end of the three parts of Game Plan Selling (Connect, Disqualify and Case Study Presentation). You've now learned how to think, act and present to your advantage during any selling situation.

As you use this system more and more, you'll find it gets considerably easier with practice. Don't be afraid to have a script for every single part of selling. You don't have to be creative; just follow the system.

Rule #40: Have a script for every single part of selling.

It's time to begin to use your new Game Plan Selling system today. The following section will prepare you to test out your new approach, by developing your Prospecting Playbook.

Have your Prospecting Playbook

...and live by it.

CHAPTER 13

Your Prospecting Playbook

Getting better at sales is just like improving at any sport. If you just show up to the game and play, you'll never improve. In fact, that's the ultimate recipe for failure. Optimism has its place, but what is most important is that you have a clear and effective playbook to follow that you can practice during the week with militant discipline. Then, when game day comes, you won't have to think at all. You'll be ready.

> ## Rule #41: Create a clear and effective playbook and follow it consistently.

You can't expect sales to come to you. You need to get out there and utilize your Prospecting Playbook. This section of the book will walk you through the two key elements of a great Prospecting Playbook.

THE AVERAGE SALESPERSONS' DAILY STRATEGY SESSION

First off, the five most important prospecting activities are:

1. **Cloud calls:** Make cold calls only to prospects in the highest relevant positions,

2. **Introductions:** Referrals are often ineffective; introductions are what will fill your bank account,

3. **Selling deeper:** Sell more by providing more value to current clients,

4. **Targeted networking:** Develop relationships that lead to business, and

5. **Speaking to sell:** Give speeches as an expert to find prospects.

Rule #42: Your goal is to maximize your return on time invested in prospecting activities.

Eventually, all five of these prospecting activities will be in your Prospecting Playbook. We'll explore more in-depth why each of these activities are so important. I'll also explain how to best accomplish each one. In the end, it will be up to you to determine which activities give you the best results and are worth your time. Your goal is to fully maximize your return on time invested in prospecting.

Besides these five activities, your Prospecting Playbook will also include your day-to-day routine. Gone are the days of waking up in the morning and asking yourself, "What should I do today to generate sales?"

Client Case Study:

One of my longest client relationships is with a high-end landscape construction company. This company sells landscape construction services to homeowners in some of the wealthiest towns in America. Their typical project will sell at anywhere between $20,000 and $500,000.

When I first met John, the president and owner, over six years ago, he had seven salespeople generating a total of $6 million per year. Because the company had been around for over fifty years (John had bought the company twenty years prior), they had a reputation in their market as a leading provider. For the past twenty years, business had simply rolled in the door. The seven salespeople really never had to do any prospecting.

Then, right before I began working with John, the market changed. Not only did the economy screech to a halt, but the housing market plunged. What was once an obvious investment in home value was suddenly a luxury that many couldn't afford. Home and landscaping improvements were likely not going to increase the value of the home at an equal level to the money put into the project. John explained to me early on how it all seemed to happen at once. What was a loud and high-energy office one day was deafeningly silent the next.

The sales team didn't know what to do. They were paid on commission, and needed to continue making money, but they had no idea where to start. Pressure mounted as fewer and fewer leads trickled in. Their initial solution was to lower prices, but that depleted their once-large margins and didn't lead to more sales. Their place in the market had seemed so solid; they were comfortable in their role as an industry-leading, high-end company. Now that they were losing business, they struggled to keep up high-value appearances in a lower-value position.

The company told the salespeople to start calling old clients to try to "drum up business" — but the efforts were haphazard. Salespeople would call clients "when they could," spending most of their time designing proposals. Enough calls weren't being made. The team's morale suffered as the stress continued to build. There didn't seem to be a solution in sight.

John was hurting tremendously when I met him. He knew what his company was doing wasn't working, so I developed a plan to zero-in on three key elements:

1. Make sure the "right" salespeople are on his team,

2. Teach the team a systematic approach to selling, and

3. Develop Prospecting Playbooks for all of the salespeople to follow.

For our purposes right now, I will not go deeply into the first two areas of focus. Suffice it to say that as soon as the team began using the Game Plan Selling system, they instantly began converting more sales.

What's most important to note in this particular case is that I developed a unique Prospecting Playbook for each salesperson. First, I taught the salespeople to get introductions from clients, do targeted networking to establish strategic relationships with other suppliers, and sell more to their enormous lists of clients.

For each salesperson, I created a Prospecting Playbook that consisted of a specific number of prospecting activities to be done each day. These prospecting activities took priority over all other responsibilities. Each salesperson was to ask a certain number of current clients for introductions, contact a specific number of people about possible strategic relationships, and call a predetermined number of former clients every single day. These were all activities that allowed for high return on invested time for the salespeople. Each day, they did the exact same things, following their Prospecting Playbooks.

The way we determined each salesperson's specific numbers for each activity was by determining what each salesperson wanted to earn. Each salesperson came up with this number on his own, just as you will shortly. This process linked the salespeople's personal goals to their prospecting activities.

From there, we worked backwards. We determined how many sales, on average, the salesperson needed to make each month in order to hit his yearly commission goal. Once we had that number, we estimated how much of each activity the salesperson had to do daily (i.e., how many old clients he had to call each day) to reach that goal.

Once the salespeople had these daily activity goals, they knew exactly what they had to do in order to hit their numbers. There was very little pushback on this because they felt empowered by having a clear Prospecting Playbook.

In this case, all of the additional prospecting only created an additional hour of work per day for each salesperson. But after implementing the Game Plan Selling system, each salesperson reported saving over three hours a day, as they were no longer chasing and putting together proposals for unqualified leads. This meant a net-gain of two hours per day. In the end, sales increased by over thirty percent over the next year. John was thrilled with the increase in sales, and the salespeople were excited about their bigger commissions, more free time, and less stress.

Crafting your own Prospecting Playbook means identifying activities that make sense for your selling situation, and determining how much of each activity you need to do in order to achieve your personal financial goals. Some tools I've have found particularly useful for this process include Google Docs spreadsheets for tracking activities and Salesforce.com for a more robust tracking and prospecting system.

As I said before, I want to take the time to explain each of the five different prospecting activities in more detail. Please keep in mind that not all of these will be perfect for every reader. On the other hand, some people will find that all five are critical to their success. Be open-minded as you read through the ins and outs of each.

But first, let's get into the prospecting mindset.

Your Prospecting Mindset

Your Prospecting Mindset: Jealously guard your time.

When it comes to your Prospecting Playbook, you should jealously guard your time. Many salespeople spend their day without planning how to maximize their time. It's this mindset that ultimately leads to a lack of a sense of urgency—and a lack of a sense of urgency leads to wasted time.

First, it's important to establish what you're worth on an hourly basis to your organization. This is going to require some very simple math:

Your Hourly Rate:

How much revenue did you personally bring in through sales last year (or how much do you realistically expect to bring in this year)? This is your annual sales figure. Write it here:

$_____

How many hours do you work in an average week?

_____

Multiply the number above by 50 weeks ([# of hours in your workweek] x 50). What does that equal?

_____

This is the total number of hours you work in a year.

Now simply divide your annual sales figure from above by the number of hours you work in a year ([annual sales] / [# of hrs you work in a year]). What does that equal?

$_____ / Hour

You've just calculated your hourly rate to your company. It's probably much higher than you might have imagined. This means that your job as a salesperson is to maximize each hour as much as possible. Wasted time checking emails, calling prospects who will never work with you, or grabbing lunch with anyone who invites you out, must become a thing of the past.

The five activities we are about to explore are all about maximizing your return on time invested in prospecting. If someone wants to meet with you but you know it will be a waste of time, then don't do it. Wasted time costs you and your company thousands — maybe even millions — of dollars.

> # Rule #43: Figure out which activities will maximize your return on time invested; add those activities—and only those activities— to your Prospecting Playbook.

Which prospecting activities you ultimately use depends entirely on your situation. I'll start with the Cloud Call—not because it's most effective, but because it sets the foundation, conceptually, for many of the other prospecting activities.

Let's begin.

CHAPTER 14

Cloud Calls

C loud Calls: Make cold calls only to prospects in the highest relevant positions.

Most salespeople are uncomfortable with cold calls. Nobody enjoys making them. I can always identify dishonest people in a room of salespeople by asking who loves to make cold calls. Inevitably, some people will raise their hands —

Rule #44: The majority of salespeople make cold calls to people in the lowest level positions because they feel more comfortable talking to people with little authority.

---

they're liars.

Cold calls are not fun. They are hard. No matter how good you are at making cold calls, you will still get hung up on, cut off, and rejected frequently. It's a tough racket. I have made more of them than I care to count, but I've also made a lot of money by making cold calls.

Low-level prospects provide salespeople with instant gratification because they're happy to waste a salesperson's time, but they rarely ever buy.

DO YOU SELL AT THE HIGHEST REASONABLE LEVEL?

If a salesperson sells widgets to manufacturers, for example, he may call anyone with the title of "buyer." This is a huge mistake. Selling to a buyer is *hard*. These folks are inundated with calls all day long and they're the savviest when it comes to handling salespeople. Often, they aren't even the economic buyers — they usually need to get permission from their bosses just to change vendors.

Salespeople should be calling people in the highest positions relevant to the sale. In some cases, it might be the CEO; in others it might be the VP of operations.

This is called Cloud Calling because you're aiming up toward the clouds rather than down into the mud. I know it sounds intimidating, but it works.

Let me show you.

I explained earlier how, when I first began selling, I went from gas station to gas station selling my services. While gas station owners are, in fact, decision makers, they would often have to apply for supplementary money from the oil company to purchase my services. In many cases, for example, ExxonMobil would reimburse a franchisee (gas station owner) for half of the money he spent on a grand opening promotion.

So there I was, banging my head against the wall, selling at the lowest level possible for years. Mind you, the owners of gas stations are very busy people. They can also be some of the toughest people to sell to. Just think, if you made your living selling seventy-five cent candy bars and one-dollar bottles of water, you would hold your money pretty close to the vest. I made some sales, but it was hard work and I could only sell one promotion at a time this way. I was getting an extremely low return on the time I invested in prospecting.

Then I learned a new way of selling. A mentor of mine told me to start calling at much higher levels. I was skeptical. I told him I didn't know where to find these people and that they were probably really busy and wouldn't want to talk to me. He ignored my sad pleas and challenged me to do it. I was apprehensive, but I accepted the challenge.

As soon as I did, I immediately realized how effective it was. I had always wanted to expand my promotion business to work with fast-food chains but had never done anything about it, so I figured that maybe this would be a good opportunity to try my experiment. This way, even if I failed miserably, I wouldn't be risking any contacts with the gas stations that were my bread and butter.

I'll never forget that experience. I was in a new Subway Sandwich Shop in Worcester, Massachusetts and I struck up a friendly conversation with the franchisee. After a few minutes, I asked him if they had done any grand opening promotions for his store. He said they didn't do much but he wished that he had. I asked him if he knew someone at Subway corporate who might be in charge of that kind of program. He told me to hold on as he grabbed his cell phone.

Within three minutes, I had the name of the VP of experimental marketing for Subway Sandwich Shops. This guy was *the* guy in charge of experimental marketing for all 3,000 U.S. locations. A one-hour cold call and two face-to-face meetings later, I was being paid to test out a brand new concept for grand openings at Subway stores.

Getting such a huge client ultimately allowed my brother and me to sell our business. Those Cloud Calls that led to our work with Subway had an incredibly high return on time we invested.

It's time for you to Cloud Call. It takes just as much time and effort to call high as it does to call low. And even more surprising is that it's usually easier to get a high-level person to talk to you. They have way less work to do than those in lower-level positions. People at the highest levels are lonely. Because they're so isolated, they don't get as much interaction. And they get sold to less, because people at the lower levels usually handle that *stuff*.

Even if you call a CEO and she tells you that she doesn't handle sales decisions, you can ask her to connect you to the appropriate person—and the CEO knows better than anyone else who that is. Plus an introduction from the CEO is very powerful.

Rule #45: Always call as high up as is relevant. Period.

Cloud Calls are the only effective way to cold call. It's simply not an efficient use of your time to cold call low-level people.

Although my audio, corporate training and Platinum Coaching programs deal more thoroughly with call technique, I want to dedicate a small portion of this section to basic call structure. Below is an example of a call made to the CEO of a $300 million manufacturing company with fifty salespeople:

(By the way, with a company this small, I would never want to speak to an employee lower-level than the CEO. Even the VP of sales or sales manager at a company this size rarely has the authority to bring a sales coach in. I will first try the CEO multiple times, either before 7:30 a.m. or after 6 p.m. CEOs work much longer hours than their receptionists. Therefore, the most productive hours to prospect CEOs is either before or after the standard 8:30 a.m. to 5:30 p.m. work day.)

My Call to the CEO:

CEO: "Hello, Dave speaking."

Marc: "Hi Dave, Marc Wayshak calling [pause for a second as if you expect him to know you], it sounds like I caught you in the middle of something. [pause]

CEO: "Actually I am busy, but I have a second. What's up?" [Prospects will often rescue you when you assume they are busy. It's a knee-jerk reaction for them to say something like, "That's okay, I've got a minute."]

Marc: "I'll tell you very briefly why I called and if it's not a fit, just tell me and we can hang up. Okay?

CEO: "Okay."

Marc: "I am a sales coach that works with mid-sized* businesses to create a game plan for selling. My clients come to me when they are losing too many sales to low-cost competitors, struggling to hit their quarterly revenue goals or getting inconsistent results from their sales teams**. Do any of those issues ring true to you?"

CEO: "Actually, we have been struggling to hit our revenue goals this past year."

Marc: "Tell me a little bit more about that."

CEO: "Well, it's been a tough year overall and the sales team keeps…"

Next I would take the CEO through an abbreviated Disqualification Checklist to see if he's a qualified prospect. If he is, I will suggest we set up a meeting during which I take him through the Game Plan Selling system.

*I don't have to tell him about the other types of clients I have, just his type of business.

**I gave three challenges that would relate to a CEO of his size company. Think back to your Opening Play.

Rule #46: Follow a script during Cloud Calls.

If you want to call a high-level prospect but don't know who the particular contact is, there are a few very simple strategies. First, go to the company's website. Almost all company websites will have the names and titles of the executives. If not, go to LinkedIn.com and do an advanced search with the company name and you can narrow the results by title. Once you have the person's name, you can call the company's main number and use the dial-by-name directory. JigSaw.com is another great resource. For a small fee, you can often get someone's direct contact information.

The point is, with a little creative effort you can get the contact information for *anyone*. And by calling high-level people either really early in the morning or after-hours, you can often get through.

You want to have a script for every call you make. When I make a call like this, I have a script to look at. I don't care if it's my 37,452nd cold call—I am always looking at a script. Type up or write down your script and stick to it.

CHAPTER 15

Introductions

Introductions: Referrals are often ineffective; introductions are what will fill your bank account.

Depending on where you are in your career, Cloud Calls may not be one of your highest-priority activities. But in any case, introductions must be a major part of your sales strategy.

First, let's clarify why I love the term "introduction" and dislike the term "referral." It's very simple: referral is just a vague buzzword in the sales world. I can't tell you the number of times I've asked for referrals only to get a letter of recommendation.

However, when you ask for an introduction, there is no question about what you want. We're in the business of getting introductions. Stop asking for anything else. What I've found is that clients are happy to introduce you to others if they have received value from your relationship.

It is a no-brainer to ask clients for introductions. Happy clients know other like-minded people, so it should be easy to grow exponentially if you have a solid client base. So why aren't most salespeople getting introductions?

THE UNREALISTIC SCENARIO THAT SCARES
SALES PEOPLE AWAY FROM ASKING FOR INTRO'S.

Fear.

Most salespeople have a subconscious fear that clients will get angry or annoyed if asked to make an introduction. This is unfounded and is costing most salespeople a substantial amount of money.

Rule #47: I expect my clients to introduce me to everyone they possibly can. So should you.

I have asked for thousands of introductions in my career. And do you know how many clients I've lost because of it? None. It's time to get past the irrational fear of asking clients for introductions. Just think of how much business you've lost just this past year by not asking every single client and business associate you know for an introduction.

I expect my clients to introduce me to everyone they possibly can. Of course, in most cases, a typical client knows less than four ideal prospects for me, but that's not bad. Let's explore the math.

If every client of mine introduces me to two solid prospects per year and I close sales with half of those people, I will essentially double my business every year by merely asking for introductions.

When it comes to introductions, there is only one word you really need to know: "help." When people that we like and care about ask us for help, we want to help. When you ask your satisfied clients for help, they'll want to help you, too.

Just like in the Connect phase of Game Plan Selling, you need to be authentic. Here's an example of how I ask clients for introductions:

Marc: "Dan, do you feel like I've provided a lot of value for you?"

Client: "Oh yeah, Marc. It's been an amazing experience working with you."

Marc: "I'm so happy to hear that. What have you found most valuable?"

Client: "Before working with you, I really struggled with selling. Now, I feel like I really have control of the sale. Plus my sales are way up…"

Marc: "That makes me feel great. I'd like to ask you for some help."

Client: "Of course, what is it?"

Marc: "The single most important way that I grow my business is by providing so much value to my clients that they want to introduce me to others I might be able to help. Would you be willing to introduce me to some people that you know?"

Client: "Of course. But I'll have to think about who would make sense."

Marc: "Would it be helpful if I gave you an outline of my ideal client?"

Client: "Yes, definitely."

Marc: "Okay, my ideal client is…[Be as specific as possible here]…do any people come to mind?"

Client: "I can't believe I didn't think of this before, but my two golfing buddies would be a great fit."

Marc: "That sounds great. Would you be willing to call them up and see if they'd take my call?" (Note: An email is acceptable as well with a Cc to you, but a phone call is always stronger.)

Client: "No problem."

Marc: "Amazing. I can't tell you how much I appreciate this. When do you think you'll have time to speak with them?"

Client: "I could call right now and give you a call back in a few minutes."

This is a conversation you can have with every single one of your clients. Of course, not all clients are going to be able to introduce you to the right prospects. Some don't know enough people. Some are too shy. Some don't like you enough. But some of your clients—many of your clients—will. This simple technique can increase your sales drastically right away.

Moving forward, you want to get in the habit of asking for introductions all day long. Even prospects and acquaintances—of course, you won't use that same exact script as above, but you adjust it to fit the situation.

A few years back, I met one of my top clients through a prospect who wasn't a fit. At the end of our meeting, we decided that her company wasn't going to invest at the level that was necessary, so we amicably decided not to move forward.

Rule #48: If you're not asking all of your clients for introductions, you're letting money slip through your hands.

However, at the end of the meeting, I asked her if she knew anyone else at companies like hers that might be a fit—and she did. I asked her if she'd be willing to see if the contact would take my call. She picked up the phone right then, called him, and then handed me the phone. We scheduled a call for later that week, and a month later we began our first project. The moral of the story is that you should ask everyone for introductions.

Of course, the best time to set the stage for introductions with clients is at the very beginning of a relationship. My policy is that immediately after I close a sale, I explain to my new client that I intend to provide so much value to him that he'll want to introduce me to his friends and colleagues.

In fact, I even hand the new client a sheet describing my ideal client. This way, the client knows what to look for.

The key to getting introductions is *asking for them*. In the end, don't worry so much about exactly how you ask—just be sincere, ask for help, and do it frequently. It's a necessity.

CHAPTER 16

Selling Deeper

Selling Deeper: Sell more by providing more value to current clients.

Every salesperson has an asset. And most of the time, it's an undervalued asset. That asset is the current client.

Rule #49: The more you can sell to the clients you already have, the easier it is to generate sales.

Unfortunately, many salespeople out there—and I've certainly been guilty of it at times myself—are always thinking about where the next client is going to come from rather than where the next *sale* is going to come from.

Where the next *client* is going to come from is a question of prospecting, precluding you from potential additional sales you could make from within your already-existing customer base. Where the next *sale* is going to come from includes your current customers in the list of possible candidates that can buy more of your services. The more you can sell to the clients you already have, the easier it is to generate sales.

Let's dig into the math a little bit and calculate the cost of acquiring a new client. Following up on an example I discussed earlier about John's landscape construction company, let's imagine that a prospect calls into the office and ultimately becomes a client. How much did John's company invest in order to acquire that new client?

Well, let's imagine that new client found John's company through one of the many marketing efforts the company employs. I happen to know that they invest about $200,000 in total marketing expenditure geared toward acquiring new clients. If they bring on fifty new clients from that investment, which is realistic, then they have paid $4,000 up front for each new client ($200,000 / 50 new clients = $4,000 spent per new client).

The cost of a salesperson's time to close the sale with a new client can range all the way up to $5,000. That means the company spent a total of about $9,000 to bring in just one new client.

That's a lot of money. Have you calculated what it costs you right now to acquire new clients? It's probably a lot more than you think. Let's figure it out.

Marketing Cost to Acquire a New Client:

A. Total cost of marketing geared toward acquiring new clients in the past year: $_____

Labor Cost to Acquire a New Client:

B. Percent of time you and/or your salespeople spend prospecting, meeting with new prospects, working on presentations, and following up with prospects (all new sales activity) in the past year: _____% (Note: if you are a salesperson, this number should be close to 100%; however, if you are an entrepreneur, this number may be lower.)

C. What was the annual labor cost for you and/or your sales team (total amount, including base salaries, commissions and benefits)? $_____

D. Now multiply line B by line C (remember that B is a percent): $_____

E. Now add line A and line D together: _____

This is your total expenditure for acquiring new clients.

F. Number of new clients acquired in the past year:

_____

Finally, divide line E by line F: $_____

This is your approximate cost for bringing on each new client.

I imagine that you're looking at a pretty large number. The Game Plan Selling system will help you shrink it. Your clients are going to perceive you as an advisor and resource rather than just a provider of the features and benefits of your product of service.

It's time to stop defining yourself only by your product or the service you currently provide. Present yourself as the person to whom your clients can turn in order to solve their problems.

This means picking up the phone and having open and frank conversations with your clients about their challenges. You can use the same exact questions in the Disqualify Phase of Game Plan Selling. Take your existing clients through that same process.

When you do this, one of two things (or both) is going to

Rule #50: Current clients are the greatest wasted assets of most salespeople.

---

happen. You might discover that your client is not fully satisfied with the product or service that you are currently providing. This is an amazing opportunity to right the wrong.

The other thing that may happen is you will identify some challenges that you can solve with other products that you sell or can create. Selling more products to a good client is one of the easiest sales that can be made. You have already established trust with the client, so helping that client in different ways is logical.

Change your mindset from always finding new clients to providing as much value as possible to your current clients. If you already have a range of products and services that you can sell to your current clients, great. If not, create them based on the feed-back you get from conversations with your current clients.

This section wouldn't be complete if I didn't share with you two best practices I've learned from clients along the way.

I've had a number of clients who sell a particular product and struggle to think of other products that would be a compli-mentary fit for their clients. Worry no more. It doesn't have to be a product. Maybe a service would offer the most value to your cli-ents. Many companies that sell a product or a range of products have a particular expertise. Think about what expertise you have that you can offer to your clients on a consulting basis.

There's a plethora of information on the Internet, but ex-pertise is one of the scarcest resources to come by in today's world. If you can identify a specific hurt that your clients are con-sistently feeling, then you have identified a tremendous oppor-tunity to help them on a paid consulting basis. Don't be afraid to tout the value of your expertise. There is a saying that one of my mentors once told me that has always stuck with me: "Expertise that is obvious to you may be worth a lot of money to someone else."

Chances are you're a wealth of information to your cli-ents — you should be paid appropriately for that information.

Providing a subscription service to your clients is another best practice. This can be a relatively lower-fee service that will provide consistent value and keep you closely connected to your clients.

For example, John's landscape construction company of-fered a tree and plant spray service that would protect clients' yards from insects and disease. This relatively low-fee service —

under $1,000 per year—had his company working on clients' properties multiple times per year.

Even better, part of the service included a face-to-face annual review with the salesperson at the client's house. This meant that the salespeople were essentially being paid to conduct annual sales meetings with their best clients. During this meeting, they could also identify new issues in the yard.

Rule #51: Create a subscription service and offer it to all of your clients.

When I first began working with this company, only one-third of their clients were part of this program. One of the first changes we made was to make this program a mandatory part of each sale—a one-year subscription to the program was now included automatically.

Another good example is Danny's Internet marketing company which, like many companies in that field, was in the business of selling large contracts that would end at a specified time, after which they would try to sign the client up for a new project. This was an uncertain process. Instead, we created the "Internet Marketing Maintenance Program."

With this program, clients would pay only a few thousand dollars per year to have Danny's company regularly test their Internet marketing strategies. Each quarter, Danny's company would present clients with a strengths and weaknesses report of their Internet marketing efforts. It wasn't a lot of work for Danny's company to do this—as low-level people could collect all the data—but it was tremendously valuable to the clients.

Moreover, it meant that Danny's company was conducting a meeting with their best clients every quarter. As a result, they were always on their clients' radar. The clients were delighted to have these reports and Danny was able to re-sell his clients on new projects more easily and consistently.

Rule #52: It's time to get away from the old-school mindset of only finding new clients.

Even if a client chose not to renew a large contract with Danny's company, they would often continue with the Internet Marketing Maintenance Program. This meant that the company stayed relevant and was more likely to get work down the road.

What type of a subscription service can you offer to your clients? Remember that it's all about getting regular face-time with your best clients. Now that you see yourself as a trusted advisor, how can you provide more value that ultimately allows you to sell more?

In today's competitive world, it costs too much money to only find new clients. Game Plan Selling is all about the greatest return on time. How can you sell more deeply to your best clients in a way that is both providing incredible value, keeping you closely connected and making you a lot more money?

CHAPTER 17

Targeted Networking

Targeted networking: Develop strategic relationships that lead to business.

I cannot tell you how many networking lunches I had early on in my sales career that went nowhere because I was willing to sit down with just about anyone. Those types of random networking meetings are just an excuse to pretend like we're doing something productive; in reality we're just hiding from our real prospecting activities.

On the other hand, targeted networking can be one of the most effective ways to generate both short-term and long-term sources of business. Yet, as with any other aspect of selling, you must have a game plan.

ARE YOU VALUING YOUR TIME?

Meeting with just anyone is simply not strategic and will waste more time than you can afford to lose. Remember what your hourly rate is—make the absolute best of every working hour spent. Let's explore how to ensure that your networking is highly targeted.

There are two important components to networking: where to network and how to do it effectively.

Where to Network

There are two places to consider for networking: where your prospects are and where people that know your prospects are. Both can be excellent options for developing a network. There is no right or wrong answer in terms of where to start. The key is that you approach this challenge with the goal of maximizing your return on time invested in networking.

When I first began my career as a sales coach, my biggest strategy for finding prospects was speaking to audiences of company executives that would ultimately hire me to train their sales teams. In order to book those speeches, I connected with meeting planners and people who put on conferences. So, in a sense, my initial clients were meeting planners, and I networked accordingly.

I started by asking my prospects where they networked. This, by the way, is one of the simplest strategies for finding great networking opportunities—just ask your ideal clients and prospects. After doing some research and checking out a few different associations, I decided to get involved with two organizations.

I joined the National Speakers Association (NSA), which is a group of speakers that present to companies and organizations around the world. I committed myself to the New England chapter of NSA, regularly attending meetings. There were two compelling reasons that made me want to invest my time and energy into this association.

First, there were people in NSA who had businesses I wanted to emulate. It became an excellent place for me to find mentors, people that could advise me on how to grow my business.

There were also many members in this association that knew the meeting planners with whom I wanted to connect. My goal was not to sell anything to anyone in NSA, but rather to get connected with the prospects that the members knew personally.

The other association I got involved with was Meeting Planners International (MPI), an association for meeting planners. This association, unlike NSA, was where my prospects were. I made it a point to go to as many MPI New England chapter meetings as I possibly could.

This is highly-targeted networking for me because almost everyone at one of these events could hire me in some capacity. Even the vendors at MPI could hire me or at least connect me with people who could.

Now that you've seen examples of two types of places to network—where your prospects are and where people who know your prospects are—what are some ideal places for you to target?

What you want to avoid are networking opportunities or associations where mostly low-level people go to socialize. Just as with Cloud Calls, you want networking opportunities that provide you access to high-level people that can either make the decision to buy from you or introduce you to the person who can.

How to Network Effectively

Once you've established *where* you're going to network, the next step is to figure out *how* to network. To be clear, there is not one silver bullet on this topic, but there are some best practices when it comes to maximizing your return on time invested in networking. Above all, when it comes to any type of networking, you need to have both short-term and long-term goals.

Short-term goals are often underappreciated. Many networking groups will tell their members that it's all about being involved for the long-term. This is simply not true.

Before a salesperson even shows up to a networking event, he should have a very clear goal of what he's going to do at the event. Whenever I go to a networking event, I set a specific goal for myself of how many people I intend to meet, depending on how long I intend to be at the event. Even more specifically, I will identify the types of people I want to meet.

For example, a typical goal for a Meeting Planners International meeting would be to connect with ten different meeting planners. At an NSA meeting, my goal would be to set up a lunch with a specific speaker who might be able to introduce me to high-level meeting planners. Whatever the networking opportunity, I have a clear short-term goal I want to accomplish.

Usually, longer-term goals revolve around becoming a trusted provider of services to the members of an organization or the people most likely to refer business to you. This often takes time. The key here is to be around consistently and maybe even get involved as a volunteer.

Rule #53: Volunteering in professional organizations can become very time-consuming if not done cautiously. Closely monitor your time invested

---

If done properly, getting involved with an organization can be a great way to get more face-time with your mentors, prospects or sources of introductions. Always jealously guard your time, and if you start to see that your effort is exceeding what you're getting in return, then it's time to reassess.

If you want to volunteer somewhere with no expectation of getting something in return, then get involved with charities or nonprofits outside of work. Having said that, my experiences with volunteering on well-chosen committees have given me tremendous access to key personnel. Now that I've helped them out, they are more than willing to help me out, too.

Working the Room

Let's be clear—networking isn't easy. There's nothing more stressful than walking into a room full of strangers with the expectation that you have to approach them. I still feel overwhelmed the first second I walk into a networking event where I don't know anyone. However, I have learned to be effective at networking with a few very simple strategies.

Your Goal: Walk into the room with a goal—but make sure it's realistic.

If I'm about to attend a networking event with hundreds of possible prospects, I want to know how much time I'll have to complete that goal. For example, let's say there's a cocktail hour before the event's speaker comes on. Then after the speech, there's another half-hour before the event ends. That leaves me with a ninety-minute window of time to network.

In ninety minutes, a realistic goal would be to meet and connect with ten prospects. I make a promise to myself that I won't go home until I have the contact information of at least ten people. There are no excuses or exceptions here. I don't particularly enjoy networking, so if I let myself off the hook I know I will never meet my goal.

Warm Up: The first three people will be the most difficult to approach.

Once I'm mentally and socially warmed up, networking becomes much easier. The second I walk into an event, I strike up a conversation with the first person I see. Every fiber of my being is usually telling me to go to the bar, but that's the worst thing I can do—it will just waste time and keep me stuck inside my own head.

It doesn't matter if the first person you talk to is the bellman at the conference center; just strike up a conversation. Follow your first conversation with two more random chats. (These don't count towards your goal, by the way—cheater.)

Conversation-starter: What you say to start a conversation doesn't matter; what matters is that you start the conversation.

Having said that, there's one line that I find to be very effective at striking up conversations at networking events:

"What brings you to this event?"

If you have something else that you like to say, great—but don't get caught up on *what* to say.

Ask the first question: After starting a conversation, you always want to try to ask the first question. Of course, if you do get asked what you do before you have the chance, just use your rehearsed Opening Play. But ideally, before you get to talking about what you do, you want to ask the person, "Who are you looking to meet at this event?"

Rule #54: Don't get creative when it comes to starting conversations. Stick to what works.

Depending on how the person answers your question, you'll be able to quickly determine whether this person is worth your valuable time to continue speaking to.

With that question you also automatically shift the focus toward the other person. Remember, most people are terrible at networking and only care to talk about themselves. Also, pay attention to what people tell you so you can make a connection. If you're the only person making connections at the very start of a networking event, you've just moved yourself to the top of the social food chain in everyone's eyes — people will notice that.

Your Opening Play: Eventually, the person is going to ask you what you do. Like I said earlier, when this happens you'll use your Opening Play — but you'll tweak it just slightly. My Opening Play at a networking event goes like this:

"I am a sales coach who works with mid-sized* businesses to create a game plan for selling. Today, I'm looking to meet CEOs who are losing too many sales to low-cost competitors, struggling to hit their quarterly revenue goals or getting inconsistent results from their sales teams."

*I don't have to tell him about the other types of clients I have, just the types of businesses that would be at this event.

If the person I'm talking to is a CEO with those problems, she'll tell me so. Then I'll take her through an abbreviated Disqualification Checklist. If she's qualified, I'll recommend that we set up a meeting or a phone call. We can exchange cards, too. All that matters is that I have her information.

When networking, never just give out cards with the expectation of getting a call back. That's a total waste of time.

Get Help from Connectors: If you talk to enough people at an event, you will eventually find a "connector." These are the people who know absolutely everyone of importance. When you come across a connector, add one more step: ask them for their "help." Here's exactly what to say:

"I'm new to this group and I'm not great at networking. Do you think you might be able to help me connect with some people?"

I've had connectors walk me around from CEO to CEO all night, introducing me to everyone.

Rule #55: Connectors enjoy doing what they do best—connecting people. Love these people.

Be sure to get the connector's information and follow up with a hand-written card and email. Work to develop relationships with these people. If they like you, they can change your world.

CHAPTER 18

Speaking to Sell

Speaking to Sell: Give speeches as an expert to find prospects.

There is simply no better way to establish yourself as an expert—and do it on a grand scale—than by speaking. I can imagine that many people are skeptical about this, so let's explore it a little bit.

Do you know more about your product, service or industry than your prospects do? I certainly hope so. You have valuable information that they want, and I'm not talking about the features and benefits of your product. I'm talking about the *real* expertise that you have.

Let me give you an example of a coaching client of mine. I mentioned earlier that I had a client named Ben who sold high-end kitchen cabinets. His average sale was about $50,000 until we met and he had acquired most of his clients through networking with groups like Business Networking International and his local Chamber of Commerce. He struggled to grow his business after the first two years.

When we met, his company was thumping along at about $500,000 per year, which was half the revenue he believed his company should be generating. Ben immediately loved Game Plan Selling because of the control it gave him over selling situations. But after a few months of working together, I knew there was more he could be doing to secure qualified prospects.

When I suggested that he begin giving local talks on how to make your kitchen beautiful, he pushed back hard. Ben was really nervous about the idea of speaking in front of a group. I explained to him that there were so many people out there who simply hated their kitchens but didn't know where to start to make their kitchens look beautiful. After much back-and-forth, he agreed to try the concept out.

We worked together to create a short presentation that he could give to audiences—based on his expertise, not on his products.

The presentation addressed the most common areas of hurt that people have about their kitchens. In his presentation, Ben talked about one client who wouldn't have dinner parties because she hated her kitchen and about another who would eat out because she hated cooking in her ugly kitchen.

The presentation was intended to last anywhere from fifteen to forty-five minutes. It was full of anecdotes, it included funny pictures of ugly kitchens on the projector, it gave some very simple but good content and, most of all, it reminded the audience that they needed to update their kitchens. It was the perfect sales tool that established Ben as the expert.

The last and most critical step was that, at the end of the talk, he offered a free five-page checklist of "what you want to think about before updating your kitchen." Ben would hand out a simple form to collect names, email addresses and phone numbers of those who wanted the checklist or to talk with Ben later on to discuss their kitchens.

There was no "sales pitch" — it was a win-win for the audience and for Ben.

After a little bit of practice, Ben began calling small groups like rotaries, garden clubs and other local networking groups. Within a few weeks, he was booking a speech per week. They were all no-fee speeches, but he was getting some outstanding leads from them. (Notice how I said "no-fee" instead of "free." "Free" implies a commodity and your expertise is anything but a commodity.)

After a few more months, speaking was his primary tool for prospecting. It was so effective because it not only provided him with strong leads, but also gave him the image of an absolute expert.

Key Components of Speaking to Sell:

Get over your fear of public speaking: Most people who don't take advantage of public speaking to generate leads do so out of fear, which is simply not a good reason to ignore one of the best tools you have to find prospects.

When I first began speaking to groups, I was very nervous about it. In fact, I was scared to death. If you have any fear of public speaking, the best way to get past it is to practice. Join a local Toastmasters chapter (check out www.toastmasters.org) and get as much practice as possible. Not only will you become a better public speaker, but you will also build self-esteem by improving this area of your professional life.

Identify expertise that your prospects want: In Ben's case, prospects wanted to know how to make their kitchens beautiful. What expertise do you have that your prospects want to learn from? I've never met a seasoned salesperson who doesn't have a high degree of expertise in something, so no excuses.

Craft your speech: This is often the hardest part. I work extensively with my coaching and training clients to help craft and perfect their speeches. Below is the basic structure every speech should have:

1. Opening story: a case study

   a. Tell a story about a client of yours who has dealt with challenges to which your audience will relate;

    b. This opening story should last no longer than three minutes;

2. Establish the main one to three points your speech will address

    a. If your speech is fifteen minutes long, you only have time for one point;

    b. If your speech is forty-five minutes long, you have time for three points, but no more;

3. Discuss your first point

    a. Give at least one useable tip;

4. Do the same with points two and three

5. Close with one of the following:

    a. A final brief story tying together your points;

    b. A quote tying together your points;

6. Offer to send your audience a special report, checklist, eBook, or article via email

    a. Hand out a simple form asking for names and email addresses;

    b. Be sure that the form asks if they'd like to schedule a meeting or phone call;

        i. Leave a space for phone numbers and best times to call.

The key is that the speech is informative, includes some engaging stories, and focuses on challenges your audience likely faces. By the way, the special report or article you offer to your audience can be anywhere from 500 to 3,000 words. It doesn't have to be anything fancy. Just give them some solid content.

Helpful tips to making a solid speech:

➢ Once you've written the speech, get a little practice in front of friends and family,

➢ Use a PowerPoint presentation, but don't jam lots of words onto the slides. The slides should have, at most, a few very simple bullet points and lots of pictures,

➢ Keep it simple, and

➢ Remember that your goal is not to be hilarious and incredible, but to identify qualified prospects. A qualified prospect won't care that you were super-dynamic. He will only care that you know what you're talking about.

Finding places to speak: Identify where your prospects will be and then get booked to speak there. You probably already know exactly where your prospects are—they'll be in many of the same places you're planning to network. Come up with a list of different groups and organizations your prospects might belong to.

Get booked to speak: Many salespeople get tripped up trying to book speeches. They believe that they need a fancy website with lots of videos and flashy buttons. The truth is, you don't need anything other than a one-page PDF document that states three things:

1. The title of your speech

2. What your speech is about

3. Who you are and what you do

That's it. If you have a nice digital photo of yourself, include that in the document, too. Once you begin to book some speeches and it becomes a serious opportunity to create business, then you can get fancier with a flashy website and professionally designed brochures.

At the beginning, just focus on creating your speech and booking talks. Keep it simple. Feel free to check out my website, www.MarcWayshak.com, for ideas on how to market your speaking.

Once you have the PDF outlining your speech, it's time to begin contacting the list of organizations you put together. This is pretty simple. You just start calling the people that run the events and tell them that you're an expert on your topic. Ask them if they ever bring speakers in to talk about that subject. If so, offer to email your information along. Follow up over the next few days.

> # Rule #56: Speaking to sell is a little work-intensive up front, but once you get going, the rewards are huge.

This is not the same type of sales call that we've been talking about up until now. In fact, it's really a marketing call. Remember, the person booking the event just wants to book a speaker who isn't going to make him look bad. So, in this case, you want to have a very simple conversation to determine whether he has any interest in booking you to speak.

Once you become more established as a speaker, these calls will get easier. But, for now, start by making your speech marketing calls and getting those first few speeches booked.

By being up there on stage, you become *the* expert on your topic to the audience. Once you've really honed your speech, qualified prospects will come flocking. And the clients who do come out of this prospecting activity will treat you like a true expert. They'll be easier to work with, introduce you to more people and gladly pay you more money than any of your competitors.

CHAPTER 19

A Note on Marketing

This is a book about selling, not marketing. However, that doesn't mean that I'm not a huge believer in marketing—I am. I love marketing. It has been an

---

Rule #57: Take advantage of the many powerful, low-cost marketing technologies at your disposal.

---

enormous part of my success.

I love that sending out a simple postcard can get prospects to call and email me. I am tickled when I get phone calls from companies that found me through a Google search. I feel fantastic when I learn that someone who saw me at a speech two years ago and signed up for my email list has been reading my emails every week.

However...

If you really want to learn about marketing, then you should find other resources than this book.

There are many books out there that can help you create the perfect marketing strategies to generate leads. Some areas of marketing that I recommend you learn more about include:

> **Search Engine Optimization (SEO):** Using your website, blogs, and online content to make Google and other search engines "like" you and hand-deliver you prospects,

> **Pay-Per-Click Advertising:** Creating campaigns on search engines, where you pay for top placement every time a prospect clicks on your advertisement,

> **Social Media Marketing:** Using sites like Facebook and LinkedIn to gain a following and ultimately convert followers into clients,

> **Lead Nurturing:** Using techniques such as weekly email tips to provide good content to prospects who may not be ready to buy from you at the moment,

> **Direct Mail:** This lost art still works if you're creative, consistent and targeted to attract new prospects,

> **Public Relations:** Getting the media to take interest in you, your company and your expertise to gain exposure to prospects, or

> **Trade Shows:** Getting a booth at a trade show to showcase your products or services.

Many sales trainers downplay marketing and act like it's not a real way to find prospects. I could not feel more differently. Especially in this day and age, marketing *must* be a part of your mix. Not exploring your marketing options is just as bad as not asking clients for introductions—both leave money on the table.

CHAPTER 20

Create Your Prospecting Playbook

Developing your Prospecting Playbook is discussed last in this book not because it's least important, but because it's a culmination of everything you've learned thus far.

> ## Rule #58: Every goal in selling must be personal if it is to be compelling.

In fact, creating your Prospecting Playbook will be the single most important thing that you do to instantly change your sales results. This simple tool will provide you the daily and weekly structure necessary to achieve your goals.

Why Every Salesperson Needs a Playbook

In sports, there is a common misconception among fans that athletic prowess is all about innate talent. But if you ask any world-class athlete what was most important to her success in sports, she'll tell you that it was practice, not talent.

Similarly, selling isn't about the one moment when you close a deal; it's about the hundreds of phone calls you make to get a few promising leads; it's about the dozens of networking events you attend to make a few solid connections. And at the end of the day, sales is a game of numbers and prospecting activities.

There is no such thing as a professional goal in sales. Every Cloud Call you make, regardless of whether it leads to a sale or a dead end, brings you closer to achieving what you want in your personal life. Every activity you complete in your Prospecting Playbook is for one purpose: to put money in your bank account so you can create the life you want outside of work. This process is powerful and personal. It will be the difference between just going through the motions and doing everything you can to make each sale.

This section will require that you write and do a little bit of math. A calculator will be helpful. Because this may require more space, feel free to do the following exercise on a separate piece of paper. This is the most important exercise you will do for your career this year.

Your Prospecting Playbook:

Because this can be confusing, I'm going to give a very basic example after each question, just to show the math:

A. What do you want to be able to have in your personal life over the next year? Write out in as much or as little detail the life you would like to create for yourself and your family. What will you buy? What do you want to achieve personally over the next year?

Example: Jen wants to move into a new house in the next year, take her family to Disney Land for Christmas vacation, and put $10,000 into her kid's college savings account.

B. How much will all of those additions to your life cost you? Estimate a dollar figure:

$_____

Example: This will cost Jen an additional $20,000.

C. How much do you have to earn in order to support your goals? Calculate what your total annual pay (bonus + commission + salary) must be:

$_____

Example: Jen will have to make a total of $100,000 in order to be able to afford all of this.

D. What do you have to sell this year in order to earn that much money? Given your compensation structure, calculate what your total annual sales must be to earn what you need:

$_____ This is now your annual sales goal.

Example: Jen is an all-commission salesperson with no base salary and she earns 10% of every sale she makes. Therefore she must sell $1,000,000.

E. What is your average sale, approximately, in dollars? Ballpark what an average sale is for you:

$_____

Example: Jen's average product sale is $20,000.

F. How many sales do you need to make this year to hit your annual sales goal? Divide your annual sales goal by your average sale ([line D] / [line E]):

_____ Sales This Year

Example: $1,000,000 / $20,000 = 50. Jen must make 50 sales this year to hit her goal.

G. In order to make one sale, how many initial sales meetings do you need to conduct? This is obviously going to be an estimate:

_____ Initial Sales Meetings

Example: In order to make 1 sale, Jen probably has to set 4 initial sales meetings.

H. How many sales meetings must you set up this year in order to hit your goal? Multiply the number of sales you must make this year by the number of meetings you need in order to make a sale ([line F] x [line G]):

_____ Meetings This Year

Example: [50 x 4] = 200. Jen must set up 200 sales meetings this year in order to hit her goal.

I. How many sales meetings must you set up per week in order to hit this goal? Divide the number of sales meetings you must set up this year by 50 ([line H / 50]).

_____ Meetings Per Week

Example: 200 / 50 = 4. Jen must set up 4 meetings per week in order to hit her sales goal.

You must set up this number of meetings per week in order to achieve your goals.

Now that we know how many meetings you must set up each week, it's time to figure out how much of which prospecting activities will get you to your goal.

Here are some of the prospecting activities related to what we've discussed:

- ➢ Cloud Calls
- ➢ Introductions
    - ✓ Asking clients for introductions
    - ✓ Asking other people for introductions
- ➢ Selling Deeper
    - ✓ Client Calls
    - ✓ Client Meetings
- ➢ Targeted Networking
    - ✓ Events attended
    - ✓ Networking connections made
    - ✓ Trade shows attended
- ➢ Speaking to Sell
    - ✓ Speeches given
    - ✓ Calls made to book speeches
- ➢ Marketing Efforts
    - ✓ Only focus on efforts that you directly manage

Now, using the list above and your own ideas, make a list of all the key prospecting activities you must do regularly:

Prospecting Activity # 1_____

Prospecting Activity # 2_____

Prospecting Activity # 3_____

Prospecting Activity # 4_____

Prospecting Activity # 5_____

Now estimate how many times you must, on average, perform each activity in order to set up one meeting. (For example, you might need to make **100 Cloud Calls** in order to set up **1 meeting**, or you might need to ask for **5 introductions** in order to actually get **2 introductions** in order to set up **1 meeting**.)

Number of Times You Must Do Prospecting Activity # 1 in order to set up one meeting: _____

Number of Times You Must Do Prospecting Activity # 2 in order to set up one meeting: _____

Number of Times You Must Do Prospecting Activity # 3 in order to set up one meeting: _____

Number of Times You Must Do Prospecting Activity # 4 in order to set up one meeting: _____

Number of Times You Must Do Prospecting Activity # 5 in order to set up one meeting: _____

Now that you know how many times you must do your prospecting activities, it's time to match those numbers with the number of meetings you must set up each week. This is where you're going to have to figure out your own mix.

I will continue with the example of Jen, so you can see how this works: Let's say that this is Jen's list of prospecting activities:

Prospecting Activity # 1_____ Cloud Calls _____ (she figures she must make 200 Cloud Calls to set up 1 meeting)

Prospecting Activity # 2___ Asking for Introductions _ (she figures for every 5 introductions asked for she gets 2 introductions which lead to 1 meeting)

Prospecting Activity # 3 Networking Events Attended (she figures that at every networking event she attends, after following up on her prospects, she'll set up 1 meeting)

Prospecting Activity # 4___ Calls to Book a Speech _____ (she figures she must make 100 speech calls to book 1 speech; and after every speech she gives, she sets up 2 meetings)

Now Jen determines that in order to achieve her 4 sales meetings each week, she must:

➢ Make 200 Cloud Call.........................1 Sales Meeting

➢ Ask for 5 Introduction.........................1 Sales Meeting

➢ Go to 1 Networking Events...................1 Sales Meeting

➢ Make 50 Calls to Book a Speech...........1 Sales Meeting

Now, to get her day-to-day activity goals, we just divide her weekly goals by 5.

Therefore, each day, Jen must:

➢ Make 40 Cloud Calls

➢ Ask for 1 introduction

➢ Make 10 calls to book a speech

She must also make sure that she attends a networking event once a week.

Jen has now identified exactly what she must do each day and week in order to achieve her $100,000 earnings goal. She now has a crystal clear Prospecting Playbook.

Your Day-to-Day Prospecting Playbook:

Daily Goal for Prospecting Activity # 1 is: _____

Daily Goal for Prospecting Activity # 2 is: _____

Daily Goal for Prospecting Activity # 3 is: _____

Daily Goal for Prospecting Activity # 4 is: _____

Daily Goal for Prospecting Activity # 5 is: _____

Note that some prospecting activities are not daily. For example, it might make sense to only go to one networking event per week. In that case, just have a weekly goal for that prospecting activity.

Now it's time to begin to track your prospecting activities on a daily basis. You can track your prospecting activities on paper, in an Excel sheet, in a Google Document or however else you'd like. It's important to keep track of exactly what you're doing each day in order to get closer to your goals.

As you begin to follow and track your prospecting activities, you might find that your ratios will change from what you originally expected. In that case, you can simply adjust your daily activity goals to reflect the new numbers. This is not a one-time process. I recommend that you recalculate your Prospecting Playbook regularly as your goals and sales abilities change.

Be sure to hold yourself accountable and, ideally, have someone else hold you accountable to your prospecting activities. I hold all of my clients accountable, but I also encourage them to

---

Rule #59: What gets tracked gets done.

---

have an "accountability partner" who also holds them accountable. Find someone to hold you accountable and go get it done.

CHAPTER 21

Parting Words

Not too long ago, I met a tech entrepreneur named Brian. Brian had passion and drive but he simply didn't have an effective plan for his sales efforts.

During our first conversation, he told me that he knew he needed help. He had a solid product but struggled to sell. He wasn't able to identify good prospects. He felt constantly under water, like many entrepreneurs do—he was juggling the responsibilities of selling along with all of the other roles he played within his company. Worst of all, he had a sixteen- year-old son and his biggest fear was that he wouldn't be able to afford his son's college tuition.

As soon as I began coaching Brian, he was a man on a mission to turn his company and life around. Now that he had a game plan, all he had to do was follow through. With his Prospecting Playbook to guide him along, it was simply a matter of doing the things he knew he had to do.

Within just five months, he brought on two very large clients, immediately doubling his business.

This is not the story of every client I work with. In fact, I tell Brian's story because he is exceptional. Even with Game Plan Selling in place, Brian's business could have continued to falter. But he followed the system without exception and that made all the difference.

As in sports, a coach and a plan can only do so much. In the end, the player himself has to find the drive and commitment to follow through and create an outcome of success. Brian's drive and hunger is what pushed him to follow every last bit of his Prospecting Playbook to the 'T.'

So, live by the *Game Plan Selling DSP* by being:

> **Distinct** from the competition, being

> **Systematic** for every aspect of selling, and having a

> Prospecting **Playbook** to live by.

If you do, you will see an immediate change, but it will only take you so far.

Like Michael Jordan once said, "Some people want it to happen, some wish it would happen, others make it happen."

Go make it happen by pushing yourself self in all aspects of selling. And, if you do, you will find your own sales greatness.

If You Haven't Yet...

As a special bonus for investing in this book I'd like to give you access to a special one-hour audio program, developed to supplement the material in this book. It's packed with information about how to immediately implement Game Plan Selling into your career and will enhance the value of the book you are now holding in your hands. Just go to www.GamePlanSellingGift.com to claim your free MP3. (You'll also receive my weekly Email Sales Tips as another bonus.)

You'll discover:

- Why being distinct from everyone else is the key to explosive sales growth in today's market
- How to instantly set yourself apart from the competition in the eyes of your prospects
- How to connect with your prospects
- How to become a systematic seller
- How to gain the respect of your prospects so they stop hiding, cheating and stealing from you
- How to give unforgettable presentations that prompt immediate decisions from your prospects
- How to create your own prospecting plan that will guarantee the achievement of your sales goals
- How to sell more than you ever have before

Claim your free bonus MP3 at: www.GamePlanSellingGift.com

The Rules of Game Plan Selling

Rule #1: In the age of the well-informed prospect, information selling is dead.

Rule #2: When you are perceived to be like every other salesperson, the protective walls of the prospect go up.

Rule #3: Times are different in today's market and salespeople must adapt or die.

Rule #4: Whether or not you sell with a system, prospects will always buy with a system.

Rule #5: Prospects will cheat in order to gain any advantage with salespeople.

Rule #6: Most salespeople will jump at the opportunity to be abused and cheated by the prospect. Don't let it happen to you.

Rule #7: The solution to winning more sales is painfully simple: Be distinct.

Rule #8: When you're a high-fee expert, clients treat you infinitely better than when you're begging to give your information away.

Rule #9: Think of yourself as a doctor, rather than a salesperson.

Rule #10: You don't want to persuade everyone to buy from you; you want the right people to buy from you.

Rule #11: Rather than persuade, identify where your prospect hurts.

Rule #12: There's no more "making stuff up" when you're in a selling situation. It's all about being systematic.

Rule #13: People are no more born with the skills to sell than they are born with the skills to play golf.

Rule #14: There is no room in sales for improvisation.

Rule #15: Every prospect expects to be qualified; no prospect wants to be disqualified.

Rule #16: People don't buy from people they like; they buy from people who understand them.

Rule #17: Most sales trainers will tell you to dress to impress. Dressing to impress may actually hurt your chances of closing a sale.

Rule #18: Match the "right you" to the prospect.

Rule #19: Realistically, at least fifty percent of your prospects will not be a good fit for your services.

Rule #20: Great salespeople do not get compliments from prospects; they get orders.

Rule #21: Ninety percent of what's in a salesperson's pipeline is pure junk.

Rule #22: People hate a sales pitch, but they love buying stuff.

Rule #23: Hurt you can solve + money to invest = qualified prospect.

Rule #24: Know what challenges you solve and only help people with those particular challenges.

Rule #25: Identify what the challenges are costing a prospect in actual dollars.

Rule #26: If a prospect isn't hurting personally due to a problem, he won't put in the effort to resolve it.

Rule #27: The person who needs your product or service the most is the one who can't afford it.

Rule #28: It's time to start asking about the prospect's budget.

Rule #29: Avoid giving presentations to non-decision makers.

Rule #30: A prospect does everything for a reason, and you can never assume you know what that reason is.

Rule #31: Always answer a question with a question.

Rule #32: It's not your job to read minds. Just ask.

Rule #33: Almost all salespeople are using the "feature and benefit" selling technique. Stop.

Rule #34: You and your services will immediately seem higher-value to the prospect when you ask them good, meaningful questions.

Rule #35: Have a repertoire of case studies that appeal to a prospect's hurt.

Rule #36: It's not about price; it's about rescuing clients from their hurt.

Rule #37: Keep your presentations short and sweet.

Rule #38: Always close with the question: "What would you like to do next?"

Rule #39: If you were strong in the beginning, the end is the easiest part of the meeting.

Rule #40: Have a script for every single part of selling.

Rule #41: Create a clear and effective playbook and follow it consistently.

Rule #42: Your goal is to maximize your return on time invested in prospecting activities.

Rule #43: Figure out which activities will maximize your return on time invested; add those activities—and only those activities—to your Prospecting Playbook.

Rule #44: The majority of salespeople make cold calls to people in the lowest level positions because they feel more comfortable talking to people with little authority.

Rule #45: Always call as high up as is relevant. Period.

Rule #46: Follow a script during Cloud Calls.

Rule #47: I expect my clients to introduce me to everyone they possibly can. So should you.

Rule #48: If you're not asking all of your clients for introductions, you're letting money slip through your hands.

Rule #49: The more you can sell to the clients you already have, the easier it is to generate sales.

Rule #50: Current clients are the greatest wasted assets of most salespeople.

Rule #51: Create a subscription service and offer it to all of your clients.

Rule #52: It's time to get away from the old-school mindset of only finding new clients.

Rule #53: Volunteering in professional organizations can become very time-consuming if not done cautiously. Closely monitor your time invested.

Rule #54: Don't get creative when it comes to starting conversations. Stick to what works.

Rule #55: Connectors enjoy doing what they do best—connecting people. Love these people.

Rule #56: Speaking to sell is a little work-intensive up front, but once you get going, the rewards are huge.

Rule #57: Take advantage of the many powerful, low-cost marketing technologies at your disposal.

Rule #58: Every goal in selling must be personal if it is to be compelling.

Rule #59: What gets tracked gets done.

Acknowledgments

There are a few people that I would especially like to thank for making this book possible.

First, I would like to thank Brian Tracy, Suzanne Bates, Steve Shapiro, Jill Konrath, David Meerman Scott and Bill Cates. Your guidance and contribution to this discussion has been invaluable and has inspired me to write this book.

I would also like to thank some people that I haven't yet met, but have been incredibly influential in my career and understanding of sales. Tony Robbins, Tom Hopkins, Neil Rackham, Alan Weiss, Stephan Schiffman and Jeffrey Gitomer have all contributed outstanding work into the sales and business world. I hope to have the opportunity to meet all of you in the future. Mostly, I would like to thank David Sandler for creating one of the strongest sales frameworks I've ever been fortunate enough to learn. It saddens me that you passed before I entered into sales.

I would also like to thank the old team from Next Level for being my first real mentors in sales. Jim, Chris and Scott, you will always be my sales heroes.

Thank you to Stephanie Mann for being an amazing editor and fixing my always rough writing style. Your support has been everything. I also need to thank my family for both helping to edit this book and for supporting me through all aspects of my career. You are what drives me.

I would be remiss if I didn't also thank all of my clients over the years that have believed in me and taught me so much. Finally, I would like to thank all of the prospects that have thrown me out of their office, shouted at me, hung up on my call and disappeared. Your lessons made me stronger and ultimately taught me how to sell.

About the Author

Author of two books on sales and motivation, sales coach Marc Wayshak has drawn on his years of experience as an All-American athlete, professional speaker, business owner and entrepreneur to create the revolutionary Game Plan Selling system.

While studying for his undergraduate degree at Harvard University, Marc suddenly lost all of his college savings in a stock market crash. Compelled to pay for college, Marc founded a small marketing company and began to learn the ins and outs of selling—the hard way.

After three years and thousands of cold calls, hundreds of speeches, thousands of introductions and countless sales meetings, Marc had finally formed his effective selling technique. His marketing business quickly became one of the fastest-growing event marketing companies in New England, with clients such as Subway Sandwich Shops, ExxonMobil and Getty Oil. At this same time Marc served as Captain of the Harvard Rugby team and was selected as an All-American. After selling his business at just 23 years old, Marc began teaching sales to organizations both large and small.

Today, he teaches Game Plan Selling to his sales training clients and corporate audiences around the country.

Marc Wayshak is America's Sales Coach on Game Plan Selling. He shares the powerful strategies and techniques in the Game Plan Selling system through his writing and his training and coaching programs. Marc travels the world helping organizations and entrepreneurs transform their sales strategy to align with today's market.

Marc Wayshak has a Master's degree from the University of Oxford and a BA from Harvard University. He is an avid runner, snowboarder and cook.

Contact Marc about his coaching programs, sales training, speaking and sales products at: www.MarcWayshak.com.